C000179314

Superhero for Hire

True Stories from the Small Ads

William Shaw

Introduced by Jarvis Cocker

The Observer

Atlantic Books
London

First published in 2004 by Atlantic Books,
on behalf of Guardian Newspapers Ltd.
Atlantic Books is an imprint of Grove Atlantic Ltd.

1 3 5 7 9 8 6 4 2

A CIP catalogue record for this book is available from the British Library

ISBN 1 84354 316 8

Printed in Great Britain by Mackays of Chatham Ltd

Design by www.carrstudio.co.uk

Grove Atlantic Ltd
Ormond House
26–27 Boswell Street
London WC1N 3JZ

For Ellen & Tomas

Contents

Introduction

Like all the best ideas, the one behind this book is absurdly simple: to investigate the stories behind the announcements and advertisements in the Classified sections of various publications around the world. And the simplicity of the idea is also its genius – because suddenly something we were all aware of yet took no notice of (unless we were looking for a new car, a flat, rubber dinghy, lost cat, guitar, etc.) is revealed as a window on to the way that people really, really live in our world today.

The most mundane of objects (fishing tackle, old bottles, caravans) provide the entry point into a startlingly varied and fascinating set of true-life stories that are by turn strange, twisted, heart-breaking, life-affirming (you know: all those things that books often claim to be but very seldom are). They show that truth is not only stranger than fiction; it is considerably more interesting – the twists and turns of the tales related here could never have been dreamt up by even the most fertile imagination.

William Shaw shows admirable restraint in his relating of the stories – simply sticking to the facts and allowing the participants to tell us their tales in their own language. (It can be depressing to be told what to think by some talentless jerk.) Shaw's skill is that he does have an agenda, an angle (a point, if you like), but he leads you there through his choice of detail or the protagonist's turn of phrase rather than signposting it desperately in the manner we have become accustomed to on so-called 'reality' TV shows. It's the details that count – and he makes them count.

Great ideas stay with you and change the way you look at the world. After reading this book you will no longer be able to see a copy of *Loot* and think of it as a mere 'listings' magazine – you will view it as a potential *War and Peace*, a chronicle of the extremes of human existence. That's good – because that makes the world a more interesting place.

Read on.

JARVIS COCKER

Preface

'Tell me something,' she asks. 'Do you make them up?'

She's a casual acquaintance – someone I've exchanged hellos with for a few years.

She's been reading the 'Small Ads' column in the *Observer* for two years but only just realized that I was the person who wrote them.

Do I make them up? I smile thinly. She's by no means the first person to ask me this. I tell her no – the people are all real. The man selling part of a SAM missile, the woman who took a Masai warrior home, the man God told to go to Alice Springs... what's here is what they told me when I answered their advertisements. Occasionally when the story is a very personal one I change a name or disguise a location, but that's all. 'World is crazier and more of it than we think.' The people next door really can be as interesting as the ever-expanding regiment of power brokers and minor celebrities we're used to reading about in our magazines and papers.

'Only I wasn't sure if it was one of those columns people make up...'

And she mentions a few; there seem to be so many right now.

'No,' I say. All true.

1

The story with that boot

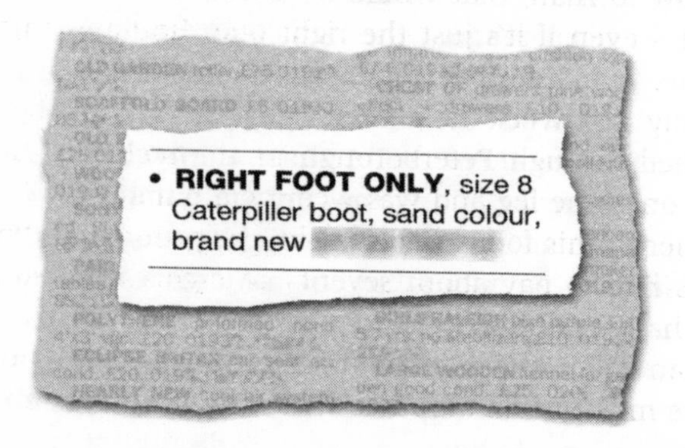

The single boot sits on the roof of the scrapyard, brand new, unscuffed and tan coloured. Alan is at the yard looking for a part for his £150 car. The thought of paying a mechanic £70 an hour to fix his car – or buying expensive new parts when you can salvage ones that are just as good from wrecked cars – offends him. Alan doesn't see the point in spending money senselessly.

'What's the story with that boot?' he asks his mate who runs the yard.

• **CASH PAID FOR LADIES USED SHOES.** I WILL BUY ALL YOUR OLD WORN OUT SHOES IN ANY CONDITION WHATSOEVER
Call me on
Between 9am and 6pm

Paul's got about fifty pairs. He keeps them in his bedroom.

'I collect them,' he says.

'I think high heels are my favourites.' Especially black sandals with high heels. It's not about the height of the heel, it's about whether it's a nice shoe.

Brown ones he doesn't like so much. When people send him a parcel of shoes he'll sort them out and sell the ones he doesn't like on eBay. There's always a few for sale online to bid on. (*'LADIES WORN & SMELLY SHOES – THESE ARE MY OWN PAIR – CAN PROVIDE A PHOTO OF ME IN THEM'* or *'Nice Well Worn Slippers Size 5'.*)

The important thing is that they've been worn. New shoes don't do anything for him. It's the idea, he supposes, that a woman has been in them.

Advertising is not just a way of buying and selling shoes. It's a way of getting in touch with other footwear enthusiasts.

In fact more or less every day somebody calls or emails Paul about his adverts. A week ago Paul got a parcel from America. Fifteen pairs at a dollar a pair – plus 28 dollars postage. He was very pleased about that package. (He always likes it if the women who send them to him include a letter, telling him a little about the items.)

True, some people do find it a bit strange, but most of the women who send him their shoes seem to understand. He's always truthful. 'I'm a foot/shoe fetishist,' he'll write. The majority say it's fine by them.

Nothing wrong with it. Same as being turned on by legs or bums, isn't it?

He's 39 now, but remembers even as a 10-year-old being aware of the power of shoes. It wasn't until he was 17 that he discovered that he wasn't alone. He says it's a bit like being gay, and thinking you're the only one, and then discovering that there are others out there too. It's like a weight off your shoulders.

One big discovery was *The Footsy Magazine* ('for foot, shoe, leg and stocking fanciers', £8 per issue), published in the Essex town of Stanford le Hope by the Foot Lovers Appreciation Society. Its website had the contact details of thousands of other British foot worshippers.

There are websites he visits too. www.trample.com. Or www.footworship.com. ('Watch these girls suck on toes like they were a lollipop!' 'She'll squish you like a bug with her beautiful arches!')

'Yeah,' Paul says, 'I am submissive.'

It can be difficult. Once he lost a girl because she didn't like the sound of it, which was a bit hurtful, but mostly they are OK with it. Women like having their feet touched anyway, don't they?

He doesn't tell his family, though. He doesn't know whether they'd understand. They'd probably think he was a bit weird.

He can't explain it. 'It's what I like,' he says, simply. 'And I'm not hurting anybody, am I?'

2

Like you, Dad

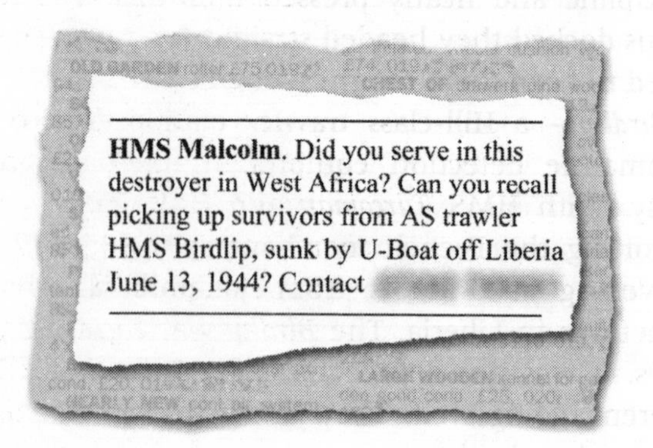

HMS Malcolm. Did you serve in this destroyer in West Africa? Can you recall picking up survivors from AS trawler HMS Birdlip, sunk by U-Boat off Liberia June 13, 1944? Contact

Around 11.30 p.m. Bill 'Nobby' Clark took a break from the engine room. It was sweltering down there. On deck, the sea was calm, the night sky cloudy.

HMS *Birdlip* was off the Ivory Coast. She was part of the Royal Naval Patrol Service – one of the small ships pressed into service during the Second World War as anti-submarine vessels and minesweepers. Navy men joked about the Patrol Service, with its converted trawlers fitted with the bare minimum of armaments. They called it 'Harry Tate's Navy' after the bumbling music-hall comedian of the time. The Patrol Service's HQ was a requisitioned concert hall in Lowestoft.

Many of its sailors were trawlermen – reservists – who had far more experience of the sea than many navy men. But they bristled at the idea of naval discipline and neatly pressed uniforms. When their ships docked they headed straight for a bar. The navy liked to keep them at arm's length.

Birdlip – a Hill-class trawler equipped with Asdic submarine detection equipment – was on convoy duty. With HMS *Turcoman* and HMS *Inkpen,* it was escorting the French merchant ship SS *Saint Basile,* travelling at 8 knots from Takaradi in Ghana to Freetown in Liberia. The *Birdlip* was zigzagging at 85 revs. It was just approaching the *Saint Basile.* Things weren't going well. They knew there were German submarines in the area.

Nobby was a stoker. He'd started by serving on the Northern Patrols, whose crews were regularly sent to chip ice from the gear to stop it building up.

Here off the African coast, escorting convoys to Durban and Cape Town, it was different. Down in the engine room the heat could be suffocating.

On deck it was dark. There was a slight swell.

At 2323 hours *Birdlip*'s radar showed something that looked like it could be a submarine at three-quarters of a mile. Sub Lieutenant Pooley, the officer of the watch, instantly called down to the captain, asking him to come up. After that, everything happened very fast.

Within a minute of the radar contact the sub was showing up on Asdic too. Radar showed it closing rapidly. By the time the skipper, Lieutenant Bradley, had emerged, Pooley could see a blur on the port beam. It didn't look like a motor launch. 'Looks too small for an ML,' he said out loud.

Bradley tried to see it too, but his eyes weren't accustomed to the darkness yet.

Pooley went to rouse the crew, but the alarm repeater bell wasn't working so an able seaman rushed round the small ship piping and shouting, 'Surface action stations!'

The ship increased its speed.

Pooley was trying to clear the ship's mess. 'Is everybody out, Chief?'

By then Oberleutnant Heinrich Niemeyer on U-547 must already have fired the torpedo. It was two days before the captain's 34th birthday. U-547 was his first command. He had spotted the ships heading on a course of N60° W, and had decided to pick off the escort before sinking the freighter, launching the torpedo from the surface.

It struck just below the bridge at 2328 hours. There wasn't much of a flash, just a loud bang. The *Birdlip* turned to starboard, heeling over to port. The ship seemed to vibrate. It righted itself a little briefly, then began to heel again, fast this time. Despite the confusion, two of the crew were brave enough to remove the remaining primers from the depth charges. Depth charges on a sinking ship would explode; the pressure from the explosion would pulverise any survivors in the water.

Next thing, those few who had survived were in the water, calling out for the life-rafts.

'Carley float here,' someone was shouting in the darkness.

Pooley could hear the captain. He sounded badly hurt.

Nobby Clark made it into one of the two floats. Few crew members had had time to put on the life jackets they were supposed to wear.

Their ship had sunk in less than a minute. The minesweepers and anti-submarine vessels of the Royal Naval Patrol Service were small. Mined or torpedoed, they sunk fast, and often with few survivors.

About five or maybe ten minutes after the *Birdlip* sank they managed to find the captain. Both his legs had been broken. They'd just pulled him out of the water when they saw a red light approaching fast. 'Quiet!' Everyone ducked down in the Carley as the submarine that had sunk them sped past at conning-tower depth, just a few yards away.

The Carley float rocked in the wake.

Then they were alone. There were sixteen survivors, including some West Africans.

In the distance they saw star shells. It was HMS *Inkpen* trying to locate the German U-boat.

Someone sang.

The captain became delirious.

Someone else pulled a barracuda out of the water and said, 'Fish for breakfast, fellows.'

By dawn they could see the Ivory Coast, five miles away. They buried the captain at sea, rigor mortis already setting in. Carley floats lashed together, they paddled towards the shore.

Demobbed after the war, Stoker Bill 'Nobby' Clark carried on with life, becoming a decorator and raising a family in Northampton.

His son Nick remembers the Remembrance Sundays when his father would turn on the television and watch the parades. He would be in tears. A teenager, Nick didn't really understand. He would go outside and play football just to get away from the house.

Though Bill Clark saw action a few times, the sinking remained the single most traumatic event of his war. He'd talk about it sometimes, but he rarely went into much detail. Nick knew why. Bill Clark couldn't help wondering why he had survived. He'd just gone on deck for a cigarette break. All his friends in the engine room died. His emotions made it difficult for him to dwell on those days.

When Bill Clark died in 1999, Nick says he found it a bit of a bombshell. He had been a great father. 'It was tricky,' he recalls. 'Yeah, it was tricky.'

Not wanting to sit around feeling sorry for himself, Nick needed something to do. It started when he read the book *Harry Tate's Navy*, written by a former serviceman.

Nick noticed an address in the book, started corresponding and the two became friends. Soon Nick was travelling to London to sift through records at the Navy Historical Branch and the Public Record Office.

It became a kind of therapy for him. 'I think I kept afloat with this,' he says.

Now it's part of his life. He is gradually filling in the details not just of the sinking of the *Birdlip* but of the other ships in Harry Tate's Navy. Now every weekend at least one of the veterans he's befriended during his research calls for a chat. Some write, trying to get in touch with old shipmates from Harry Tate's Navy. And dozens of people like him – sons and daughters, grandchildren, nephews and nieces who want to know more about their loved ones' lives – email him. It's about much more than just his father.

Every year he goes to the annual RNPS reunion at Lowestoft. His father used to come when he was alive. For a week those that are left and fit enough to travel gather, staying at an old holiday camp near by. Old men with fading tattoos. Each year there are certain faces Nick looks for and doesn't see; he doesn't ask in case he gets the wrong answer.

But there are a few younger ones; children who, like Nick, are trying to find out more about their fathers, to see whether anybody can tell them stories that will help them understand them better.

This year is the Patrol Service's twenty-seventh annual reunion. Not bad for a service that was disbanded in 1947. Patrol Service veterans think the navy was glad to be rid of them after they'd done their job, mopping up the last of the mines. But there's an incredible bond among these men. Maybe it's because they were a small service, set apart from the rest of the navy. Maybe it's because the ships they served on were so cramped you became especially close to your shipmates. You had no choice.

Nick stays with his girlfriend at a hotel in Lowestoft. In the evenings the old boys go to the Floral Hall, the old dance hall where they used to dance when they first arrived here to train on the minesweepers, or the anti-submarine ships.

With their wives or daughters, they dance to 'In the Mood' played by a DJ who, used to the tone of these occasions, has draped a Union Jack in front of turntables; he wears a Union Jack hat. The men roar the words to 'Land of Hope and Glory'; they toast the Queen with rum. They can still put it away.

'God save the Queen.'

'And us!' somebody shouts. 'And us.'

Nick is used to this patriotism. He has immense respect for the men here. He's not sure he could ever do what they did.

At half past ten on Saturday morning the men start to march slowly through the town. Sea cadets push the wheelchairs. An ambulance crawls slowly behind them.

The band of the Royal Marines was supposed to lead them, but they couldn't make it. There is a firemen's strike; they're on emergency duty.

Instead, the band of the Army Air Corps have filled in at the last minute. 'We'll never live it down,' the old men mutter. 'The day the army had to save the navy.'

The shopping crowds pause. Some look away, embarrassed at the sight of these old men, marching stiffly. A few youngsters giggle. One or two older people stand stiffly and salute. A few clap. There is a soft clinking of medals.

Traffic is made to wait. Impatient, someone leans on their horn. 'Not interested, are they? They don't realize.'

'Why aren't you marching?' one sailor upbraids another.

'Hundred yards and I'm gasping. I got angina.'

'Why don't you get in a wheelchair?'

A snarl. 'The day I get in a wheelchair, that's it.'

The first autumn leaves blow down Mariners Street as they pass. They climb up the hill to Bellevue Park above their old HQ – the Sparrow's Nest – and gather round the white Portland stone of the circular memorial that was dedicated in 1953. Above it rises a 40-foot neo-classical column. On the top sits a small gilded galleon.

A chaplain reads the service. They sing hymns; 'For Those in Peril on the Sea'. They gaze at the 2,385 names there.

> THESE MEN OF THE ROYAL NAVAL PATROL SERVICE
> DIED IN DEFENCE OF THEIR COUNTRY AND HAVE NO
> KNOWN GRAVE BUT THE SEA.

The names of Nick's father's friends from the *Birdlip* are there on the bronze panels that surround the memorial.

Hearing the words 'They shall not grow old as we that are left grow old', a grey-haired man takes off his glasses and wipes his eyes.

A bugle plays.

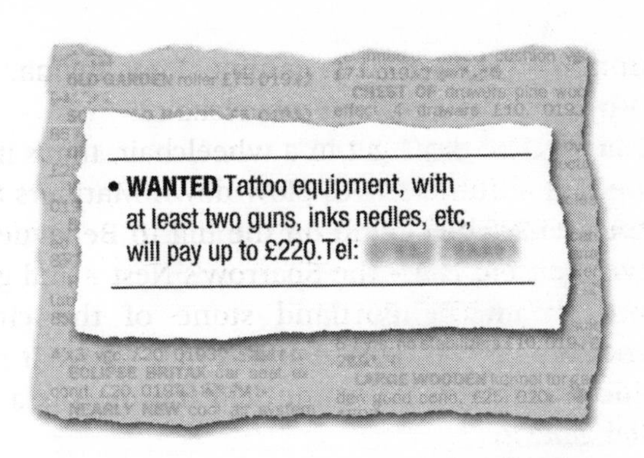
• **WANTED** Tattoo equipment, with at least two guns, inks nedles, etc, will pay up to £220.Tel:

At 18 he couldn't care less about nothing or nobody. That was when he had his first tattoo done.

'Punk lives.' It cost him a quid.

His name is Paul. Friends call him Spike. Others Sid.

When his parents split when he was about 11 he chose to stay with Dad. Which was a mistake, because Dad knocked him about something rotten. Not just slap-slap either. Once he put a hot iron on his face.

'When I get bigger I'm gonna 'ave you,' Spike used to say.

By 15, he was in care. That was around the time he got heavily into punk. One day he turned up at school wearing tartan bondage trousers and a Sid Vicious T-shirt.

Soon he had thirty or forty rings in each ear, and then the tattoos started.

He's got the Anti-Nowhere League, the Subhumans and the Misfits logos. One side of his neck it says 'LOUD PROUD AND PUNK'. On his head there's a cobweb and 'PUNKS NOT DEAD'. Both arms are covered, as is one of his legs and part of the other one.

It got him into fights.

'What the fuck do you look like?'

Which made him just want to look worse.

'Fuck you.'

He took drugs. He'd go through six or seven wraps of speed in a weekend plus loads of LSD on top of that and drink too.

He doesn't go into pubs any more. Someone always starts on him.

It took until he was 27 for him to get his own back on his dad.

His dad made the mistake of pushing him. Spike freaked. 'I'm not a kid any more!' he shouted, and punched him. Knocked him right out.

All those years he'd had it inside him.

The following year he was in the kitchen peeling potatoes when he collapsed, hyperventilating. He thought it was a heart attack.

A couple of days later it happened again. When the doctor came round he said, 'You're having panic attacks. I'm going to have to give you Diazepam.'

You're only supposed to be on them a few weeks. Spike has been on them nine years. They make him tired all the time. He stutters when he talks. Recently they've tried weaning him off them, but now the panic attacks are coming back.

A hypnotherapist said the attacks are caused by what happened to him in his childhood.

A psychiatrist said it's all the street drugs he used to take, thinks the panic attacks are just a ruse to get more drugs. Spike says, 'He doesn't know jack shit about me. What I been through.'

The way he looks doesn't help. People stare. He looks like trouble. 'VOICE OF BRITAIN' is tattooed on his neck next to a skull and crossbones. If the local tattooist hadn't moved away he'd have finished the other leg by now.

That's why he wants the equipment. To finish the job himself.

He's still a punk. Hates chart music. All love love love – care care care. They don't sing about the truth. What really goes on.

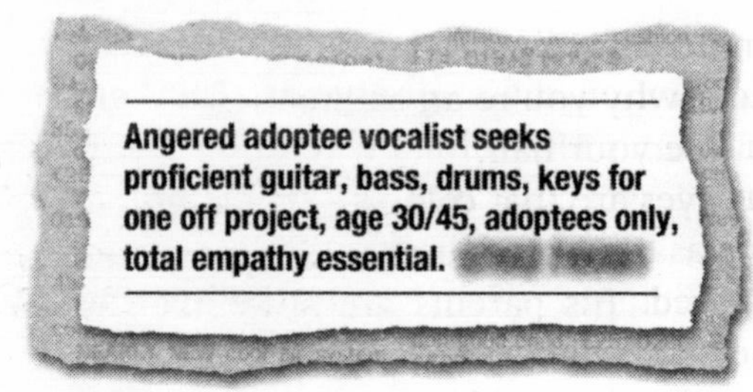

Angered adoptee vocalist seeks proficient guitar, bass, drums, keys for one off project, age 30/45, adoptees only, total empathy essential.

And so it's all gone wrong,
as you well know by now
I'm on the road to all your secrets,
and I can let them out
So, you don't want me?
I'll say I don't mind when of course I do

Away from it all,
reflect on what you've done
I'm on your mind; I'm in your heartbeat
and there's no way out
'cos a life means forever,
so take it on the chin like you're meant to do

'Some Day Soon' by Simon Clothier

When you're an adopted person you grow up not looking like people – so Simon says.

You look in the mirror and think, Where did that come from?

You examine yourself.

You wonder why you're an asthmatic.

Why you lose your hair.

Why your eyes are that colour.

For as long as he can remember his parents told him he was adopted. His parents are absolutely brilliant people. They told him about when he first came to them, six weeks old, and how he cried constantly for three or four days.

He's 41 now.

He has been looking for his birth parents for twenty years. When he was 24 he succeeded in tracing his mother. He started with six sheets of badly photocopied paperwork.

His mother had been 15 when she'd given birth to him. From the documents he knew which school his mother had gone to, and the name of the headmistress, Mrs Dunford, who'd helped organize the adoption. 'I owe that lady everything,' Simon says.

At 6.30 one night he'd called up the school and reached a cleaner who'd remembered Mrs Dunford. She was chief of staff at the ILEA now – the Inner London Education Authority.

'I knew you'd turn up one day,' she told Simon when he called her.

They met for lunch at County Hall. She recognized him in the throng because he looked like his mother.

She agreed to contact his mother to arrange a meeting.

His mother agreed to meet, and when they did she told him about why he was adopted. His father, it turned out, had been only a year older than her – 16. He had lived in the street adjoining the school. Bit of a lad. Had a moped. They got together on a coach trip to Southend. She wound up pregnant. Her parents wanted her out of the house so Mrs Dunford and her husband took him in.

At first, after they met, his birth mother treated him as some sort of special person. She kept telling him how great he was. 'Simon, you're wonderful.'

Simon found that difficult. After a year he reacted against it. 'No, this is wrong.'

She'd missed the part of his life where he'd done stupid, nasty things like throwing up on the carpet at home, crashing his dad's car at 17 when he was over the limit, or trashing the house by throwing parties when his parents were away.

He kept his distance for a couple of years after that, just staying in touch through phone calls and letters. It was as if he felt he had to be almost nasty to her, to make her understand that he wasn't perfect. It took a few years for the relationship to settle down.

But Simon's birth mother had no idea how to track down his father. What made it so much harder was that his surname was a very common one.

So Simon kept looking in the mirror and wondering. For a while he was almost a rock star. He was singer in a band called Saints Believe Us, who released an album and a couple of singles. For fifteen years after that he was in car rental.

Having children of his own prompted him to restart the search. His second was a boy, now 4. When he began to see himself in his son he started to wonder about the way things had turned out for him.

He was watching GMTV in October last year. They were running something called *Adoption Week*. Seeing it finally kick-started him.

It can take time. His search filled a file as thick as a phone book. The breakthrough happened when he chanced upon a researcher who was looking into making a programme about adoption. Amazingly the researcher became interested in Simon's case and came back with the name and address of his birth father's mother – Simon's grandmother.

Simon had always assumed she was dead, but she was living in a sheltered flat in Sidcup.

He went there on 5 November last year, armed with a bunch of flowers. He was incredibly nervous, knowing that in her flat he would, at the age of 40, see a photograph of his father for the first time.

She invited him in. He sat down and bosh – there it was. A picture of his father with his brother.

Simon felt he was looking at someone identical to himself.

Excited, he went downstairs with the phone number his grandmother had given him and called his birth father.

It was a disaster. The man he called denied everything. He couldn't handle it, thinks Simon. 'He knew I was around; he'd held me after I was born. He just never thought I'd find him.'

Simon has been in touch with one of his father's daughters – his half-sister. 'God,' she says. 'You're exactly like him. You even *move* like him.'

He left a letter for his father with his grandmother that day. As far as he knows, the letter has never been read.

In all the twenty-two years he's been looking, this last year has been the hardest. It has stunned Simon that his birth father didn't even want a conversation. That he didn't even want to acknowledge that Simon existed. He tries to think about what it must be like for him. In those days they made you sign a form telling you you were not allowed to have any contact with your child. They encouraged you to bring the emotional shutters down.

He's allowed his birth father a year to get over the shock, to get used to the idea of having Simon as a son. He's heard that one of the man's daughters has been ill;

he may have needed time to get over that too. But he's had time now. And Simon hasn't heard a thing.

Simon isn't trying to replace something he's not had. He's been lucky. He had a very happy upbringing. It's purely a case of needing to understand all the bits and pieces of his make-up. He doesn't want or expect love. He's owed a conversation. That's all. Whatever the law might say, Simon believes that's his due.

Simon thinks about his own son. Sometimes he thinks about the girls he screwed around with in his teens and when he was trying to be a rock star. Luckily he never got any of them pregnant. We're an odious species, the male, he sometimes thinks. We shag around. We think it's funny. We think there's no comeback.

He doesn't blame his father for making his mother pregnant, but there's a tab to pick up somewhere along the line. Maybe he thinks Simon is just going to go away. But if so, Simon says, he underestimates human nature. And genetics.

When he started looking again, his own father warned him of the dangers of continuing the search. But Simon hadn't expected it to be so hurtful. This last year has changed him. Disoriented him. He finds he cries a lot. He feels fragile.

Simon's wife is nonplussed; she doesn't understand how obsessed Simon has become.

He doesn't know what to do with his anger. So he's trying something. He's gone back to what he used to do in the 1980s. He's written a song. He wants to record it. Nobody else has to even hear it. But he thinks maybe just recording it may help assuage the fierce fury he now feels towards his birth father.

The chorus goes, *'You don't have to be kind/ You don't have to be there for me/ You don't have to tell me when, or where, or with whom/ Just see me again, some day soon...'*

His birth father saw him at least once when he was a baby. All he wants is to be able to look the guy in the eye once more. To see and be seen.

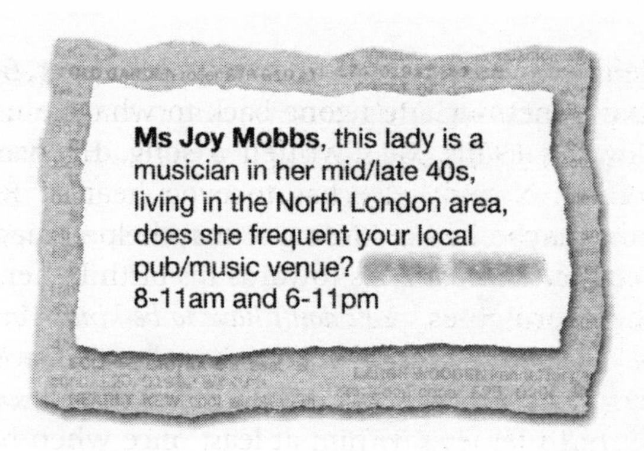

Ms Joy Mobbs, this lady is a
musician in her mid/late 40s,
living in the North London area,
does she frequent your local
pub/music venue?
8-11am and 6-11pm

A middle-aged man sits alone in a house in Enfield. The place is pretty much bare save for a TV, a suitcase, a mattress and a guitar.

Outside is a 'For Sale' sign.

When he sells the house he's going to take his suitcase and his Fender Strat and go to America. He's going to hang out with the old blues players there. Travel round the southern states. It's something he should have done years ago.

James used to live with his parents in this house. They're dead now. His father was an alcoholic; James used to swear, 'I'll never become an alcoholic like you, Dad.'

James was going to be a successful rock musician. He was a good guitarist.

He'd sit in guitar shops, trying things out.

One day in the early 1970s this guy, Steve Gannon, sat down next to him, watching him play some chord.

'How d'you do that?' Steve asked, one guitarist to another.

James showed him. Steve became his soulmate. He's never found anyone he could play with like Steve. It was like two guitars talking to each other. For a while they played together in a band called Shadowfax. They weren't very successful, playing old blues and prog rock stuff, but it was a lovely time.

James would visit Steve in his hippy cottage in a village called Stanstead Abbots. The two would play for hours. Steve's girlfriend Joy Mobbs would join in, playing bass or piano. She had a great ear.

That was it really.

The last time he saw Steve was 1979 when he disappeared to America to become a roadie.

In 1980 James was in a band called the Dharma Bums. One night he returned home after a gig, incandescent with happiness. The crowd had been great. The band had all the right contacts. The feedback they were getting was terrific. This time they were definitely on their way.

The band were taking the drums and amps out of the van, stacking them up in the hallway when James burst into his parents' room saying, 'This is it. We're going to make it. We're going to get a big house and everything.'

His father was drunk. All he said was, 'You and your fuckin' music. And all that shit in the hall.'

He really brought him down.

James stormed out, slamming the front door. Spinning round angrily, he punched the glass. It shattered.

He cut himself. It was like the inside of his right arm was falling out. He had severed all the tendons.

That was the end of the Dharma Bums.

The band members removed their gear from the hallway; none of them ever bothered getting into another band. To James it was strange. The doctors fixed his tendons, but it was as if his music career was over in a second.

James went off the rails after that. Something got hold of him. It was one addiction after another, with alcohol in the backline all the time. First barbiturates, then Valium. He tried heroin, but didn't like it – thank God.

Ironically, it was alcohol which really brought him down. Like his dad. Each time he thought he couldn't go any lower, he would. It was like being in an elevator. You'd go down, step out at one floor, then get back in and go down again, lower.

His dad died the year after he'd cut his arm up. James stayed in the same house, with his mother. He married and moved away, but addiction wrecked that, so he moved back in.

Three years ago he was drinking three, four bottles of vodka a day. Literally down on his hands and knees, crawling. He'd pass out, lying in whatever surrounded him, wake and start over. You name it, he's lain in it.

It was absolute hell.

Three years ago he decided he'd had enough. After twenty years as an addict he just stopped dead.

To celebrate, James decided to go on holiday to San Francisco. 'Oh,' an old friend said, 'Steve Gannon lives in San Francisco now.'

James called up international enquiries. There were two S. Gannons in San Francisco, and one of them was Steve. He was living in Oakland. He's a successful blues musician now. His band play Monterey every year. He has a residency in a club called Blakes on Telegraph in Berkley.

Steve invited James to play on stage with him there. It was the first time James had played live for years – sober, at least.

They jammed blues numbers on stage. James was overcome. This, he realized, was where he was supposed to be. He felt shocked. He felt ecstatic. He also felt regret for how much time he'd lost.

Back on the guitar again, he's playing better than

ever now. He's finally selling the house he smashed his arm up in and going away to start again.

When they were together, he and Steve talked about the old days jamming with Joy. They'd both lost touch with her years ago. 'But wouldn't it be nice to track her down – maybe get her a ticket to come over to San Francisco to have a good jam again?'

Back in the UK James has searched on Friends Reunited and scoured the phone directories. One old friend says he saw her two years ago at a music pub on the Balls Pond Road.

James knows why he wants them back together; it's about a time before everything went bad.

When he was out in America with Steve that time, they went to play a gig together in Nevada. Approaching Lake Tahoe on the way, they'd gone down into a deep valley. The sign read: 'Blue Canyon'.

'That would be a good name for a song,' Steve had said.

James has written the song now.

'We're going down into Blue Canyon/ And up into the break of day…' When he sells the old house, he's taking the song back to Steve as a present, for them to play together, both of them, on stage.

3

The chemistry

LESBIAN LOVEBIRDS,
3458 miles apart. 4yrs of flying, phoning, trying to find way 2B together – crippling £42000 debt. Immigration heartless.
Barclays

Someone came into the chatroom with the nickname 'Animal'.

Having just graduated in zoology, Karen tried guessing what sort of animal.

She and 'Animal' ended up swapping messages all through the night about life and the universe. They clicked. It was 7 July 1999 – the night Karen met her lover. Broke and still living in student halls, the free Internet was all the entertainment she could afford.

Debbie said she lived in New Jersey and had three children.

Online, they fell in love. After three months online every day they decided it was time to talk on the phone.

Karen's first words, shouted out loud to Debbie, were: 'Good morning America.' Debbie's children were on the other end of the line, crowded round the phone to hear the English accent.

By now, online and on the phone, they were talking to each other three, four hours a day. But soon the phone calls weren't enough. Debbie decided she was coming to London to meet Karen.

Waiting at Heathrow was absolutely terrifying. It didn't help that Debbie's flight was an hour late. A friend had offered to give Karen a lift there and had to spend that time driving round and round the airport, unable to find a parking space. Karen waited in the arrivals lounge, freaking out.

They knew each other so well – but only in the virtual world. You hear so many horrible stories about Internet relationships. In front of the real person, walking out of customs with her suitcase, Karen felt suddenly exposed. This complete stranger coming up to her and hugging her. *Whoa.*

On the journey back into London they barely spoke. Online they had never had any problems being intimate. In the flesh it was strange. 'This is a real person here.'

It took a day or two before the nervousness wore off and they both suddenly started to open up to each other. '*Now* I recognize her!' And it was great. All the chemistry was there again.

When Debbie left it was horrible. And each time it's worse. They wanted to live together, but Debbie couldn't move to England because of her children and Karen didn't want to leave London and her friends. But after eight months Karen was finding the separation hard.

One day she went to see *Angela's Ashes*. She came out of the cinema and called Debbie. 'I'm coming!' she said.

Debbie was so happy she climbed a tree in her yard, still gabbling delightedly on the phone.

Karen said, 'Get someone to take a photograph of you up there.'

Karen still has the photograph. Her lover, up a tree, talking to her on the phone.

Back then Karen thought all she had to do was make that decision and everything would magically fall into place. But while UK immigration authorities recognize same-sex parnerships, in the USA they don't.

So she went into IT, thinking this was her best chance of getting a visa – just as the dot.com bubble burst. She was lucky to get a job in the UK, let alone America. At least she had an income, and not just to fund her US trips either. The really bad news was that Debbie had been diagnosed with the auto-immune disorder lupus. She couldn't work. With two households to help support, plus the flights, Karen's debts were mounting fast.

And that's where things have stuck. Karen goes to New Jersey three times a year. Debbie lives in the suburbs of central Jersey, by the ocean. When she first went they did all the touristy things, but all Karen wants to do is hang out with Debbie and the children at her house. Sometimes they go to Vegetarian Paradise in New York.

Debbie visits the UK twice a year – 3,458 air miles, each way.

Every time they separate it's awful. Several times, driving her to the airport, Debbie has had to pull over and be sick. Back home alone, Karen becomes zombie-like – she switches off all her emotions. And then, after about a month, it all comes back and she starts to really cry.

Bush becoming President was like a knife in her gut. All hope of liberalizing immigration laws for same-sex couples disappeared.

It got worse after September 11. Since then the officials have started asking more questions. 'Why are you here so much?'

The pressure of going through immigration is unbearable. Standing in the queue waiting to approach the booth, she is anxious. She blushes. She starts to shake. She takes a deep breath and rehearses what she's going to say. She can't tell them the real reason she has come to America, because having a gay lover is grounds for refusing entry. You might overstay. And once your passport has been stamped, that's it. It terrifies her. It would be the end. Debbie is the only lover she wants.

All she can say is, 'I'm visiting friends.'

Once the officer said, 'Oh, you're coming to visit your girlfriend?'

She had to remind herself that girlfriend means a little less in America than it does in Britain.

She's going there in November for a long stay. But she's scared about what's going to happen this time. She's heard of people being put straight back on the plane home. The more red entry stamps fill her passport, the more the immigration officers will become suspicious. She's terrified they'll ask her a direct question. She'd be scared to have to lie.

When she visited a sympathetic immigration lawyer recently he told Karen her whole strategy for getting a visa through IT was flawed anyway. She should have stuck with zoology – that way at least she'd have been eligible for an H1B visa for people working in their graduate field. That's the silly thing. She never wanted to do IT; she wanted to do zoology all along.

She has wasted three years, thrown them down the drain.

She's built up £42,000 in debt, flying, sending money to Debbie. The repayments work out at £850 a month. She couldn't afford to change jobs and start again now anyway.

The lawyer said there are maybe 100,000 other gay couples like her and Debbie in the same situation. He told her about one woman who had been going back and forth for fourteen years until they found a letter from her lover in her handbag. That was it. She couldn't go back.

Karen is getting desperate. She just wants to be with Debbie and her children. It has been four years now since they first met online. Sometimes she questions why she's doing this, but she can't imagine anyone more wonderful than Debbie. She'd rather be alone than not be with her.

Debbie's sister has become ill and Debbie's looking after her three kids too. Six kids and no income. The stress can make the lupus worse.

Once they spoke on the phone and Debbie said, 'Oh my God. I feel like I'm going to die.'

She was taken into the emergency room of her local hospital. Karen was frantic, calling friends all night to try to discover what had happened. She was just about to jump on a plane when she reached someone who told her, 'She's all right.'

On dark days Karen wonders whether Debbie is going to make it through this.

Her debts are mounting. She's scared. She keeps expecting some sort of resolution but all there is is this ongoing, heart-wrenching pain.

Debbie's eldest daughter writes to politicians. 'I can't bear to see my mum sad any more. Let Karen come.'

Debbie's youngest clutches Karen at the airport. 'If I don't let you go then you can't get on the plane.' It's a joke, but Karen has to turn away. Don't cry. Don't cry.

The world everywhere seems to be opening up. There are so many ways to communicate with people on the other side of the planet. But then there's this thing, immigration.

There are all these phrases. Love conquers all. Love builds a bridge. She wonders where her conquer-all is.

There are the air miles, of course. She has enough now to be able to take a companion for free, next time she travels. Which is ironic.

• **GOLDFISH CLUB**
60th anniversary reunion dinner, Lincoln and RAF Cranwell, September 27–28. Goldfish members and paying guests welcome. For details ring

It was New Year's Eve 1942 and Maureen was at the local church hop when RAF Sergeant Jim Julian and his mates from RAF Hooton Park walked in.

'Can we get any beer here?' they asked.

'No, this is a church. We can get you a tea or a coffee.'

Maureen asked him for a dance.

'No, I don't dance. I'm not interested in dancing.' But she persuaded him, so she danced her way into 1943 with him.

After that she didn't hear from Jim. When she bumped into him several days later she asked: 'Where've you been?'

Jim said he'd been in the Irish Sea, swimming. His plane had crashed. She didn't believe a word. RAF men always came up with the biggest lies.

But then Maureen saw the piece in the local paper. *'Lifeboat rescues four men.'*

For once, she thought, an RAF man who tells the truth. But by then Jim had been posted overseas.

Jim was an air gunner. On 8 January he had been on a mission trying out an early experimental version of radar known as ASV. Air to Surface Vessel. It was very hush-hush.

They were flying in a Blackburn Botha when its Bristol Perseus engines failed. They were famous for being unreliable.

At low altitude there was no chance of bailing out. As Jim sat in his little gun cabin, the worst part was waiting for the impact. It was only a matter of seconds before they hit the sea.

And then trying to get out. Jim managed to find the small escape panel on the side of the plane. He says, 'You'd be surprised how small you can make yourself if you want to.'

The plane sank like a stone within thirty seconds, but not before the crew – an Australian, a Canadian and the two British servicemen – managed to get the dinghy out.

The Irish Sea in January was, as Jim puts it stoically, 'quite cold'. Day turned to night. It was a small dinghy and as he and the Australian were in better shape than the others they jumped into the sea and clung on to the side and swam. They didn't know what they were doing, but swimming at least made them feel useful. It was as if they thought they could swim all the way back to Wales.

Jim was 19. He didn't have the sense to know what his chances were, luckily. It never entered his head that he wouldn't be OK. 'Somebody will see us.'

After twenty hours a Hurricane spotted them and gave a waggle.

Hours later the Aussie shouted, 'There's a boat there.'

It was the lifeboat. Only when it got them aboard did Jim realize he had such bad exposure he couldn't hold the teacup they offered him. When they gave him a can of food he cut his hand and watched the blood flow out, feeling nothing.

He ditched a second time, three months later, but this time it was in the Med flying out of North Africa, and it was only eight hours before they picked him up.

They didn't have a dinghy. It blew up when they tried to inflate it. Somebody must have put the wrong size of gas bottle on it.

Instead they had to sit on the wing of the Anson, waiting for rescue.

'That's unusual,' said his mates. 'Old Jim Julian having two baths in one year.' In wartime nobody would be sympathetic about a thing like ditching: you daren't be, otherwise you'd be crying every other day.

Jim didn't even know the Goldfish Club existed until his waterproof membership card arrived in the post. He was among its first members.

The club had been set up in November 1942 by one C. A. Robertson, chief draughtsman at Messrs P. B. Cow & Co. Ltd – the company that made the life jackets and dinghies that saved ditched airmen. Robertson had been inundated with letters thanking him for their products. In response, he set up the Goldfish Club.

There was a Goldfish Club cloth badge too – a white-winged goldfish flying over two waves. Dress regulations meant you couldn't wear it on your uniform, but crews would stick it on their Mae Wests, or under the flap of their uniform pocket.

When they ran short of cloth to make the badges owing to rationing, William Hickey ran a column in the *Daily Express*, appealing for old black evening suits.

Jim made it through the war, flying seventy-two missions in all. He got four kills. Shipping strikes were the worst, going in through all that barrage. It wasn't so bad flying out on a bombing raid, but on the way back you always seemed to hear funny noises coming from the engines, see a few holes that you thought shouldn't be there. And then you'd wonder whether they'd got the landing gear. What was going to happen when you touched down?

Even then, you never thought it would be you, though.

Ten years after Robertson started it, the club held its first anniversary dinner. There were nine thousand members back then.

Those who made it to the dinner would dine on tables with goldfish bowls on them. The poor fish rarely survived the port and brandy that was poured into their bowls.

Sixty years later there are only seven hundred left, including those who've ditched more recently. The average age is about 80; few make it to the get-togethers. At 81, Jim is now chairman of the club.

He's trying to get sponsorship for a sixtieth anniversary dinner, but no one's come forward yet.

He's been married fifty-five years now – to Maureen. The local paper had printed his home address in the piece they wrote, so she wrote to his parents and they passed on his new address.

'Me ditching,' he says, 'it's how I met the wife.'

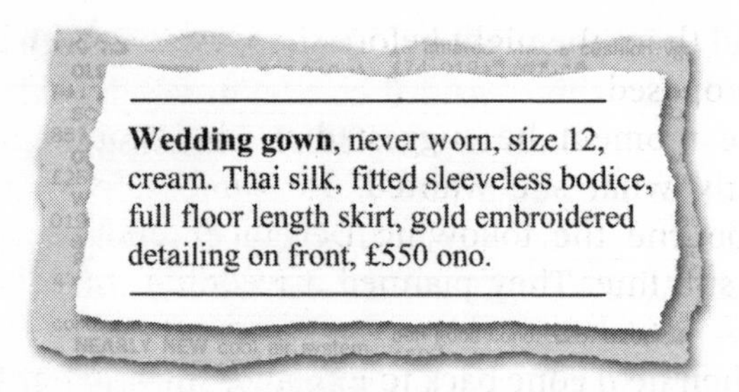

Wedding gown, never worn, size 12, cream. Thai silk, fitted sleeveless bodice, full floor length skirt, gold embroidered detailing on front, £550 ono.

It sits on top of the wardrobe in a box. For months she didn't know what she should do with it.

She arrived from Australia in '96. She loved London from the start; got a job in a Covent Garden shoe shop and discovered a great bunch of students who all hung out together. Pretty soon she moved out of her Aussie digs, into her own flat in Clapham. 'I'm really more of a suitcaser than a backpacker,' she'd joke.

The new friends were really good fun. And one was this guy Ben. Back then he was a struggling DJ, and really, really skint. He moved into her little flat, and then they got a house together.

She and Ben had been going out for about two years, but Felicity's two-year visa was about to expire. She'd built up a lot of debt living in London too, and needed to go home for eighteen months to work to pay it off. Besides, she needed time to think about what she was doing next.

And then, the night before she was due to fly home, he proposed.

The moment he suggested it, she thought it was exactly what she wanted. He came to visit her in Melbourne the following December and everything was still fine. They planned a wedding the following year.

When he'd gone back to England, she and her family began to think about what dress she would wear for the wedding. Her grandmother said she'd pay for it. She had this morbid fear of not being able to see her granddaughter's wedding dress before she died. It was silly, but Felicity wanted to humour her.

And her mother knew a young, groovy girl who was a seamstress. So Felicity sketched out a design, and the friend measured her in order to turn Felicity's drawing into a calico dress. She became swept up in it all.

Now, with hindsight, Felicity wonders why she stayed away from London for eighteen months. Perhaps, unconsciously, she was putting the whole thing off, not dealing with it.

She prepared herself for a life with Ben in London. Upped sticks. Had everything shipped from Australia – clothes, furniture, bed linen.

But when she finally arrived back in October 1998, Ben wasn't broke any more: he'd become a successful musician. It seemed as if everything had changed.

And, strangely, instead of being happy to be back with him as she expected to be, she was miserable.

They struggled to get along. They argued. After three months trying to get to grips with their feelings, Ben simply came out with it: 'I don't think we should get married.'

What hurt as much as anything was that it wasn't just some off-the-cuff remark. It was clearly something he'd been stewing on for ages.

Unprepared, she begged him: 'Don't leave me, don't leave me.' She was upset, paranoid.

So they stayed together, until a month later she turned around and said to him: 'Well, you're actually right.'

Really, she'd known it the moment she'd arrived back in Britain. And she realized she had just become caught up in the whole thing.

Ben and Felicity are still friends. She was worried about the split at first, because she knew that all her friends were his friends too. But they were fantastic about it: 'We just want you to be happy.'

Felicity is still in her twenties and in another relationship now, but it isn't fair to her new boyfriend for her to keep the dress up there in the box that it has never been taken out of.

Perhaps she will want to get married some day, and if she does she may even want a dress that's exactly the same. Just not this particular one.

• **Cheryl**. . . They say 'Say it with flowers'
But there isn't enough flowers in this
world to say how much i love you. . .
Xxx. . . Billy

Billy's been married before.

He had a lot of heartaches over that. Lost the kids. The kids came back. She took them away again. Back and forth all the time.

'I'm not doing that again,' he promised. Not interested.

For ten years he's been on his own. His lifestyle doesn't suit relationships.

Living in Morley, south of Leeds, he's a sound engineer for a cabaret group called Soul Story. Four white men who sing Motown covers in clubs, casinos and holiday camps up and down the country. Billy sets everything up for them, does the sound check, puts water on stage for them. People say, 'Oh, that must pay you loads', but it's peanuts really.

He fell into the life. For years he'd worked in an engineering factory. He came out of that and joined a courier company, up and down the country for two years – 120,000 miles a year. Swore he'd never go back into a factory again.

Then Caroline, who's been a singer all her life, asked him to help her out at a few shows. He worked for other acts, then about seven years ago started with Soul Story.

It was Caroline too who suggested he come to the Swan for karaoke night.

Cheryl was there. It was odd that they'd never met before. They live close to each other, and Cheryl is the sister of Caroline's boyfriend. She had even worked at the same courier company as Billy. They've been that close, and never met.

That night at the Swan they talked; neither of them is a singer so they didn't get up and do karaoke, just sat and chatted. She wasn't looking for a relationship, any more than he was. She'd had a really tough life. There are things that happened to her that she'll never really get over, which make it difficult for her to get along with men; but she doesn't really like to discuss it.

She's partially disabled. In her twenties she caught meningitis. Nobody expected her to live. It's left her with problems in her arms and legs. She's in and out of a wheelchair.

She was married too. Her husband never took her out anywhere. She stayed at home. In the end, Cheryl ended up raising two children by herself. Apart from that, she's never had a relationship with a man that lasted more than six weeks.

After karaoke a few of them always went for a curry; Billy and Cheryl joined them.

'So? You going to ring her up and arrange to meet her?' said his friends afterwards.

'I don't know.' He didn't want to be hurt again.

Cheryl was the same. Though she was going his way, she took a lift home along the M62 in Caroline's car instead.

When Caroline started telling him, 'She wants you to ring her up,' it took him three days to do it.

Caroline warned Cheryl he wouldn't be around much because of his job. 'That'll suit me down to the ground 'cause I never get on with fellas. They get on my nerves.'

But to the surprise of both of them, it just fell into place. Within a week he'd moved in with her. After a month he realized he wasn't going to be hurt this time.

She's the same. With other blokes she's been out with she couldn't wait for them to go; to get out of the house and leave her to her own devices. Now he'll just reach the bottom of the street and she's texting him. She keeps copies of all the texts he sends her, and insists he copies them out for her, dates and all, when she has to clear them from her phone.

When he goes away he always brings something back with him. Anything. Doesn't matter what it is. A beer mat. A broken earring. She keeps them in a box.

Amazingly it's been ten months now. Caroline called them up the other day. 'Fancy going to Benidorm? Don't worry about anything. I'm paying for it. Yes or no?'

Billy said yes. Cheryl wasn't too happy about it at first. But they're flying on Saturday – it's their first holiday. She's never been on a plane before. She's nervous.

• 2 SWF, 21, WLTM, SM (GSOH) 4 GT&L.
ASAP drunken-urban-chicks@

Sally's a Christian: she discovered her faith at school. She started going to Christian Union meetings. They were evangelical Christians and, though her family had never been religious, she came to believe that what they were talking about was true.

Her Christianity has changed since those days. She finds evangelicals too intolerant. But her faith is still as strong.

At university, she studied drama, imagining she'd become an actress.

Almost straight away, she knew that was a mistake. Everyone else on the course made her feel jaded: they were obsessed either with themselves, or with who was sleeping with whom. Some found Sally's Christianity strange.

Besides, she realized that the only people who were going to make it were those who were totally convinced of their own talent. Which she wasn't.

That's when she found out that what was really important to her was her Christianity. So maybe she should follow that as far as she could. She should be a priest.

She's a smart, vivacious woman. She likes a drink, good conversation, a laugh – a bit of titillation.

She imagined the seminary would be full of people she'd like. It wasn't. She finds the people there dull. And incredibly earnest. Every time they hear about the death of someone's mother or father, her fellow students leap on them, desperate to try out their newly learnt counselling skills. Sometimes she thinks it's silly, her training to be a priest. She's got a very low tolerance threshold for people who say they've got problems if she doesn't regard them as *real* problems.

And the other thing she quickly realized about her fellow trainees was that almost all of them were gay.

Gay and boring. The Church seems to attract people like that. Many seem to have grown up in small villages where they've probably had to hide their sexuality. She supposes that the Church offers them a profession in which the whole issue of marriage isn't important.

But she's come to believe that this generation of gay would-be priests is a massive problem. How can you have a Church of England that's supposed to represent everyone that will soon be led largely by one class of people?

And it's the utter hypocrisy, stupidity and insensitivity of the Church of England: here are a large group of people who the Church won't even accept as 'inheritors of the kingdom', yet it's letting them run its parishes.

Plus the fact that they're all gay isn't helping her love life.

One night, she and her friend Amy – who's not from the seminary – are getting drunk in a pub in Villiers Street, near Charing Cross. Right now Sally shares a place with two nuns, but Amy and Sally have decided that next year they're moving in together. Amy was at Cambridge. She came to London to work, but she too finds it hard meeting men in London.

Both are in the pub bemoaning the dire state of their love lives. That's when they first start talking about putting an ad in *Private Eye* – almost as a way of christening their new plan to move in together.

'Wouldn't it be fun if —'

'No, that would be sad!'

But they do it anyway, writing the advert for the 'Eye Love' column there and then. *Two single white females, 21, would like to meet two similar males, good sense of humour, for good times and laughs. As soon as possible.*

If Sally was seriously looking for the love of her life, she'd have mentioned her religion. This is just a giggle. Though you never know.

Now the email replies have started coming in. The first is promising. It's from a man who works in the House of Commons; he sends them a satirical poem about the election. But others arrive too.

The soldier who talks about the time his girlfriend chucked him after she caught him advertising in *Private Eye* himself for a bit on the side.

The two men who say they are so immensely fat they need help finding their penises.

The boy who describes himself as having 'Atlantic blue eyes', and the one who sends a picture of himself at his aunt's 60th birthday.

Two men who say they're Jehovah's Witnesses (she thinks they're just taking the mick).

Some are inarticulate, some over-verbose.

Sally hoped they'd have more of a sense of humour. There must be a band of men out there who desperately answer every lonely heart advert, regardless of what it says.

Sally and Amy are making up a list of possibles. They've got a file. The man from the House of Commons has sent nine more poems – mostly about politics.

Sally thinks she'll try him first.

• MASAI WARRIOR
Available to attend Functions, Weddings, Party's etc. Fully traditional dress. Greeting guests, singing, serving drinks and food. Specialist skills preparing and serving coconuts. Reasonable rates. Call

Thirty years ago, Bingwa Njoke Silongooi is born near Arusha and grows up in a Masai village. His family own cows; to the Masai living in the bush cows are everything.

Unlike others in Tanzania, Masai are allowed to carry weapons. The government encourages Masai to remain traditional – they represent the African values tourists like to see. So, in a red cowhide scabbard, Bigwa carries the long sharp knife he made himself.

At 15 Bingwa kills a lion with it.

At 16 he is circumcised. He becomes a Morani – a young warrior. As when they removed his two bottom front teeth, which they do to all young men, or thrust a burning stick through his ear lobes, there is no anaesthetic. Circumcision is part of becoming a Masai warrior. Strength is prized. You're not even supposed to blink when they cut you.

Around 1998, Bingwa travels to the Kiwengwa region of Zanzibar to become a security guard on a building site. They're building an eighty-eight-room luxury resort which is to be called the Blue Bay Hotel. All the hotel rooms will face the white, sandy beach and the ocean beyond. There's to be a luxury pool, a fitness centre, diving facilities and a floodlit tennis court.

When they finish it Bingwa stays on and becomes a watchman at the hotel. When he's not guarding he sells Masai jewellery and dances for the tourists on Sunday evenings, at the Blue Bay and at some of the other hotels in Kiwengwa. In his high, reedy voice, Bingwa sings about the lions that kill their cows, about coming home triumphant after killing a lion.

Every few months, he goes home to Arusha to see his family; when he does he's replaced by one of his brothers.

Wendy arrives with her 15-year-old daughter to spend Christmas and see in 2003 there. She's never travelled outside Europe before.

One day, with about half a dozen others, Wendy goes on a walking tour of the local village. Two

Masai accompany them; Bingwa is one of them. What Wendy is struck by, as her feet begin to ache on the 6-kilometre walk, is how courteous he is. Seeing her struggling with her bag, he offers to carry it. It's more than just a sense of duty. It's a sort of chivalry.

And he's very handsome. Looking back, she says, with a slightly embarrassed laugh, 'I suppose it just started from there.'

Wendy has lived alone with her daughter since the child was 5. In those ten years she hasn't had a single boyfriend. She never expects to meet someone like Bingwa; or that someone like Bingwa will like her. It comes out of the blue. Maybe if she were younger she would be too frightened, but she's older now and embraces the adventure.

At first, Bingwa doesn't speak English. She doesn't speak Masai or Swahili. She is in property management and letting. His only real possessions are the knife he made, a watch an Austrian tourist gave him and a mobile phone. But their differences don't seem to be a problem.

Back home, they continue to text and email each other. The British immigration authorities turn down Bingwa's application for a tourist visa because he clearly doesn't have enough money to support himself here. They don't refund the £40 application fee.

Bingwa says he's giving up his job at the end of February and going back to Arusha. Crazily missing him, Wendy flies back in mid-February to spend a week with him.

Some people tut-tut when they hear he is finally coming to the UK on a fiancé visa. 'It's like taking a lion out of the jungle and putting him in a cage.' But Bingwa's father gives his approval, warning that he must avoid fish and chicken because Masai regard them as dirty food. So Bingwa arrives in April, getting off the plane in full Masai gear.

Bingwa is adapting well, though there are occasional moments of confusion. The first time Wendy loaded the dishwasher Bingwa was shocked to see her putting dirty pans in what he thought was a cupboard. He likes to help out. He watches a little junk TV. Sometimes he does the gardening, using his sword to cut back weeds. He's discovered the World Service in Swahili on the Internet.

He's quiet, and sometimes it's difficult for Wendy to know whether he's happy or not. He's grown up in the company of men; he misses his old friends. He misses the singing and dancing, too.

Wendy wanted to help him feel he has something to do here. When an Asian friend asked whether he'd help out at a wedding in August – cutting coconuts with his sword – he happily agreed, so Wendy thought other people might want to use his services as a Masai warrior too.

He's been here two months. The visa runs only for six.

She's cautious, waiting to see how things go.

Chances are, she says a little ruefully, he'll soon tire of her.

4

A nation of prudes

WANTED 3 Guys to form 'The Four Forty Monty'. Are you 40–49, reasonably fit, up for a laugh, will get your kit off in a room full of ladies & earn a few quid. (no single guys or chippendales please) Want to give it a go call Chris/ Jayne Tel:

Watching *The Full Monty* one night a few weeks ago at their new home in Birchington, Kent, Chris says, 'I've got an idea. What if we do the Four Forty Monty?'

At first Jayne doesn't know what he's on about.

'Well, there's the Fraud Monty, isn't there?' The Fraud Monty are an Essex-based Full Monty tribute group who strip and re-enact routines from the movie. 'And I'm in my forties…'

'Yeah?'

'Well, the Four Forty Montys?' Four 40-year-olds doing the Full Monty.

For a 47-year-old, Chris is proud of his body.

'I'm in good shape,' he says. 'I've got a young body. I'm not blowing my own trumpet but people think I'm 37, not 47.'

He's not a shy person either; he and Jayne work as a husband-and-wife DJ team doing karaoke and disco. They're playing on Saturday at the Foxhunter Caravan Park in Kent where Patsy Palmer used to have her caravan.

Chris goes out under the name of DJ Thong. Behind the turntables he wears a short kilt, a sequinned top and a jester cap. When the ladies are on the dance floor having a laugh, he'll sometimes lift his kilt and show that underneath he's just wearing a thong. The older ones love it. They're always trying to take a little peek.

'I don't mind,' Chris says. 'It's all done in good taste.'

Jayne doesn't like the idea of Chris performing naked, though – not at first. She doesn't mind him showing the thong but after that it's no go.

Chris reckons it has a lot to do with the time she went to a hen night and there were these Chippendale-type men trying to shove their things in your face, or putting them into girls' hands. 'I can't see the point in that,' Jayne said. 'I'm not going to anything like that again.'

But the Four Forty Montys won't be anything like that. 'It's going to be done in such good taste you could take your mum to it,' he says.

Taking their 8-year-old daughter to school, Chris tries the idea out on some of the mums on the school run. A lot of them think it's great.

This could be big, thinks Chris.

He reasons that a lot of women are going out to see shows with these well-endowed Chippendale-type men. The guys must feel really out of it. But they wouldn't mind their wives going to see something like the Four Forty Montys. Though he's in good shape he hasn't exactly got a six-pack; in fact there's an operation scar on his stomach. He doesn't have a beer belly, but wouldn't mind if the others did as long as they were only small ones. It's the guy-next-door image.

Chris is sure that if they get it right they can make lots of money. He's got these ideas for routines – like four guys all standing in line to 'March of the Mods', jumping up and down.

'Can you imagine that? Well, it don't take a lot of imagination, does it?'

The first time would definitely be nerve-racking, but after that it would be like riding a bike.

He asks his mate Dave what he thinks about it. 'If you got the bottle to do it, then do it,' says Dave. ''Cause I haven't.'

'Would you still talk to me if I did it?'

'Course I would.'

He's already thinking about how they could do a whole evening, with maybe an Ann Summers show to start, and guest acts. Maybe even dinner. He's thinking about selling T-shirts.

The only trouble is finding the other three. No one else seems to be up for it.

Only one guy has answered the advert so far, and he's from Devon, which isn't that convenient. Jayne and the man from Devon have swapped a few emails. He sent a picture of himself. The guy's wife took it. He's standing there, naked.

He seems quite keen.

But already Chris is starting to worry that maybe he's a bit over-keen.

It is, says John, a slightly naughty thing to do.

Not naughty in any overtly sexual sense, he adds hastily. It's an impish, harmless sort of naughtiness.

The excitement of simply seeing people, men and women, naked in someone's living room, drinking coffee or a glass of wine. The enjoyment of exhibitionism and its counterpart – voyeurism.

When people first take their clothes off, the subject inevitably turns to what beaches you've been naked on and so forth. But the point is there's something different about being nude in the everyday normality of someone's house. It's the context.

It's a visual image John loves.

He wouldn't deny there's a sexual edge to it, but this is the fourth year he's been doing it and the people who come understand that it's not about anything beyond being naked in front of other people. It doesn't lead to further liaisons. In fact, many of the people who come are already in relationships. Their partners may not even know they come here.

The idea of Project Nude is that people can do something they've been longing to do, which they might have some difficulty explaining to their friends.

And of course he runs it because there's no point in being an exhibitionist without voyeurs – and – and he's a bit of both.

He doesn't charge. It costs him very little. He works from home. Project Nude is simply a second phone line that he can switch off if the nuisance calls get too much.

There are about ten to fifteen calls a day, always more men than women, of course, but this year for some reason the proportion of women has dropped. He's not sure why.

It's harder for women to go naked, John thinks. There's a lot of pressure on them to have perfect bodies.

Men and women look at each other in different ways. He has watched how women may check out a man's penis, briefly, but it's just out of curiosity. Men are inevitably more sexual in the glance. For some women that's part of the fun – the idea of being the centre of attention, even the idea, John says, of being hunted. It can be why some women have mixed emotions about taking off their clothes at his gatherings. It's not so bad if they're the most attractive woman there, but if they're not blessed with the best of looks they can feel marginalized in such naked company.

Sometimes, if it's going well, he takes things a little farther. People are asked to walk around. To be observed.

Sometimes, but only with the agreement of his naked guests, he takes photographs too. But the funny thing is, it's not really about the pictures. In fact, he rarely looks at them afterwards, and if he does he finds them really rather boring. It's about being photographed.

We are different people at different times. Different at work from how we are with our partners, or our family. And sometimes we may wish to do things they wouldn't understand.

That's why anonymity is so important.

His own included. Some friends know; others don't. His family certainly don't. If they found out, he says, they'd think he was completely mad.

The latest addition is his Saddam Hussein condom.

He bought it via the online auction company eBay for a little over £2. It's an American gimmick, produced by the same sort of people that are cashing in on the current anti-Iraq sentiment with Saddam toilet paper.

Ian buys a lot on eBay. In the Derbyshire house he shares with his wife Jo, he owns all sorts. He has condoms issued to German, American and British soldiers during the Second World War. Latex doesn't age well, so they're pretty brittle now, but he's fascinated by the little envelopes they put them in. He's proudest of the pink art deco ashtray made as a promotional item for the American company Ramses. It's beautiful. It cost him only around £20, but he's paid over £200 for rare condom tins before.

Condoms, he'll tell you, date back four thousand years. Egyptians made them out of linen, but the oldest one he has is Victorian. A reusable one made of thick rubber. They didn't even call it a condom back then, to save embarrassment. When shops stocked up with it they'd ask for 'small pencils'. And that's what would be shown on the invoice: 'small pencils'. It was all very hush-hush.

The Chinese and Japanese made them out of tortoiseshell. Must have been horrendous.

It's hard to find fellow enthusiasts. He's tried setting up a network of condom collectors on the Net. There are quite a few in America, but not here. Ian thinks that's because there's still a stigma about them here. We're a nation of prudes.

It probably dates from the 1980s, when he became a nurse. His first job was at the deep end, working with prisoners with HIV and Aids in Brixton jail. Back then there was a lot of ignorance. Many nurses wouldn't take a job working with them. Newly trained, Ian didn't share that ignorance.

It was a tough time. Shocking. Young men – apparently fit and healthy one minute – dropping down dead. That was an eye-opener. Other prisoners didn't want to go near them.

HIV-positive prisoners were placed in isolated units.

So the people who treated them – like Ian – became isolated too. Looking back, he's glad he did it. It taught him a lot about people. But it was a miserable time.

His wife Jo is a nurse, too. They met while they were both training. Ian gave up a few years ago after stress made him too ill to work. Jo still works as a psychiatric nurse, but she too wants to get out.

It was in 1998 that Jo first talked of setting up a business of her own. Ian thought the Internet was going to be huge. They discussed all sorts of plans. Sex was big on the Net, and they considered selling adult toys, but neither of them knew anything about them. Instead, they decided on condoms.

They launched in May 1999. Both were completely naive. They had no idea how any prospective buyer was going to find them on the Net. They were astonished when – four days after they went live – their first order came through for £25 worth.

Part of it was the name. Jo called the business Big Boy Condoms. She wanted something funny that would stand out. She had no idea that most of their business would actually come from men who had problems with size.

They regularly receive emails from men who are either too big, too thin or too small for the condoms you can buy in the high street.

They ask questions about their sex lives. Psychologically, it can be pretty tough for some men, thinking they're the only ones out there with size problems. Thick, thin, extra-long. You feel a freak if you can't get your size. Email somehow makes it easier for men to talk about problems.

Jo keeps her stock in two wardrobes. She says turnover doubled after their first year, and it looks like doing the same again this year.

Ian started the collection when he noticed how often the American companies were changing their display designs. There are more condom companies in America. Their market isn't as regulated, maybe.

He kept the old ones, and then began wondering what happened to all the designs he remembered from the 1970s.

Now he's collected over three hundred separate items. His fantasy: one day he'll have enough to set up Britain's first ever condom museum.

5
How to change

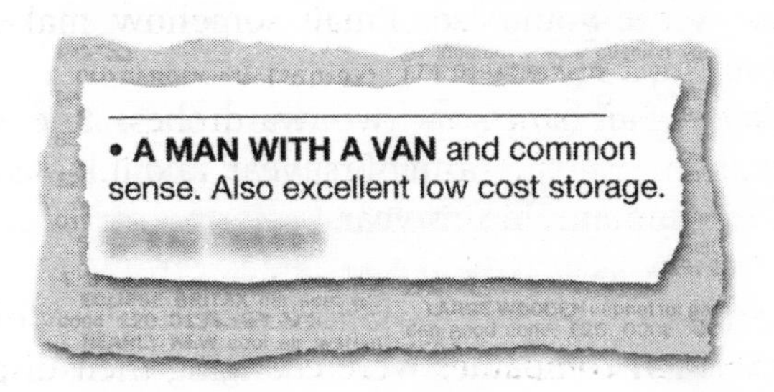

It's 8.15 on a Sunday evening and Martin takes off his shoes and is pouring himself a little congratulatory vodka for a good day's work when the phone rings. 'You the man with the van?'

Martin does removals. 'Yeah.'

'Can you come now?'

'Whoa, there. What's the job?'

The man says he wants to be picked up in Piccadilly, drop some stuff off at his girlfriend's round the corner and then take the rest of the load down to a mate in the Oval. 'OK,' says Martin finally.

'What religion are you?'

'You're drivin' me nuts already. What's the matter with you?'

'I want you to swear on your god that you'll be here in fifteen minutes.'

Turns out the guy has just been let down by another driver at the last minute. Martin tells him to take a bloody Valium and relax. (In retrospect, he later realizes, probably not the most tactful thing to say.)

Quarter of an hour later he picks up the man – name of Stephen Smith. Martin's reading Howard Marks's *Mr Nice* – the autobiography of a former drug dealer. Mr Smith looks exactly like a character from out of the book, dressed like some old-school gangster. Picking up this heavy suitcase, Martin jokes, 'Christ... this must be the drugs, then?'

Mr Smith starts laughing.

'What's so funny?'

So Stephen Smith starts telling his life story. Turns out that in his day he had been a notorious bank robber, criminal and ne'er-do-well. He was part of a gang that stole Sophia Loren's jewels. And he'd been addicted to speed for twenty-seven years.

'When you've finished reading Howard Marks's book,' says Mr Smith, 'you'll have to read mine.' He's written his own true-crime best-seller about his years on speed – *Addicted*.

A thoroughly nice man, decides Martin afterwards. Probably be a bit tasty if you got on the wrong side of him, but thoroughly nice.

It's what Martin loves about removals. The people. He doesn't enjoy driving, and certainly doesn't like humping boxes up and down stairs. But people turn out to be the saving grace.

It's weird. He's a complete stranger, but customers tell him all sorts of things. It's something to do with the stress of moving. And because they know they'll never see him again in their lives.

There was the Colombian international footballer who chatted to him about his career as he transported his cousin's belongings. And there was the call from this posh woman who said she was Lady Saunders's secretary. Could he move a chair that Wednesday, from Bishops Avenue to Worthing? It turned out Lady Saunders was the old agony aunt Katie Boyle. Stinking rich, she was, but really nice.

Martin was glad he did that job. The trip gave him a chance to visit his mum, who lived near Worthing. She was ill at the time. In fact, she died unexpectedly a few days later. If he hadn't done the job for Katie Boyle he might not have seen her before she passed away.

Driving a van has changed Martin's life. He used to play guitar for a living. Three years ago – at 45 – he realized it was time to give it a rest. But he knew he'd last about three seconds in a proper job. He was completely unemployable.

He had a van to shift his musical gear in, so that became his job instead. Before, as a musician, all he knew were people in the business – other musicians. He was in this little bubble. He was a performer: everyone else was somehow different from him. He never felt he was part of the real world.

All that has changed. Now he's just the geezer in the van. He reacts to people differently now – and they to him. He likes people more than he used to. He might only meet them for a few hours but there's an intensity about the time.

Like the prostitute who wanted him to move her adult-sized school desk and canes for her. She wasn't just some 18-year-old single-parent crack-head. She seemed to be right on top of her life.

'She was lovely,' he says. And when he'd finished the job she gave Martin a giant fluffy bunny for his kids.

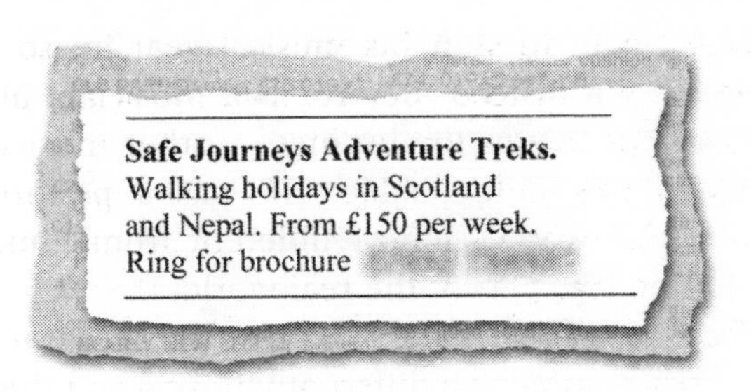

He couldn't live in a flat land. It was the mountains that drew him to Scotland as a teenager thirty-two years ago. He looks out of the window of the small tin building that serves as his office in Aberfeldy and sees Ben Lawers and Schiehallion.

It seems to Richard that he was born to climb mountains. His mother gave birth to him on the day Everest was conquered – 29 May 1953.

His father was a climber. Richard ascended his first peak, Snowdon, when he was 5, sometimes carried on shoulders. Every weekend they would climb. As a child he would look through his dad's books about Everest, at the pictures of a different world. His father had always wanted to see it, but with five children he could never afford it.

It took Richard until his late thirties before he saw it himself. He was working on an estate in Scotland when ten years of insurance contributions paid a dividend of £1,500.

'This is the money I'm going to Nepal with,' said Richard. His wife hummed and hawed. She wanted a fridge freezer; in the end she went with him.

Visiting Everest base camp, he thought back to all the stories of the great mountaineers he had read. Photographs can't capture the feeling you get there, looking at it in the thin air.

He once thought he'd like to climb the Big One. Now that's not so important. Partly because the most valuable thing he found there was not Everest itself, but the Buddhist Sherpa culture. He's changed his mind about what life is about.

He has been back every year. Once, trekking, he found himself in an isolated Sherpa village called Gankarka. The good nature of the people he found there affected him deeply. It is a place that is good for his soul.

Of the Tibetan Buddhists who arrived in the high valleys of Nepal in the 1500s, some settled in the Khumbu area, under Everest. Those Sherpas sustain their culture by helping visitors climb. The Sherpas of Gankarka village are in the more isolated Helambu district. They haven't been as fortunate. That first time in the village, Richard found its only English speaker, Dorje Sherpa, who explained how young people were drifting away to Kathmandu.

As an estate worker, Richard understood their problems. Wild bear and deer were decimating their crops, and, as Buddhists, the villagers wouldn't kill them. Farms were failing.

Richard thought of the miles of deer fences he'd dug in back home.

After a frustrating time obtaining a visa, he managed to bring Dorje here to raise money. Dorje raffled a Tibetan rug; the Rotary Club helped, too. Together they raised £2,000; not much, but enough.

That winter, Richard returned to Nepal. They had two miles of chain-link fence handmade in Kathmandu. Sixty-five porters carried it into the mountains. It was an amazing sight, each man carrying a 60-kilogram load on his back. That Christmas, Richard taught them how to erect it, cutting posts from the rhododendron trees. They've begun fund-raising for a school there, now. People have started returning to the village.

Two years ago he quit his job. His back was worn out from digging and lifting. He can still walk well. So he set up his business, taking people up into the mountains of Scotland in the summer, and, in the winter, to Nepal.

In Scotland he has lived a solitary life. Now he discovers he enjoys people, pushing them to go a little farther, seeing them open up. Most are in their fifties. They are people like him, who've always had a dream of seeing Everest.

It doesn't pay much – less than his old job. But he wishes his back had gone ten years ago.

ORDER TO SHOW CAUSE FOR CHANGE OF NAME

Case No.

Superior Court of California, County of Los Angeles.

In the Matter of Petition of: Fiona Irene Brigstocke, an adult.

It is hereby ordered that all persons interested in the above-entitled matter of change of name(s) appear before the above-entitled court as follows to show cause why the petition for change of name(s) should not be granted.

Date: 01/31/03, Time: 9:00 AM, in Dept: 1A, Room: 548, located at 111 North Hills Street, Los Angeles, CA. 90012.

It appearing that the following person(s) whose name is(are) to be changed is/are over 18 years of age: Fiona Irene Brigstocke.

And a petition for change of name(s) having been duly filed with the clerk of this Court, and it appearing from said petition that said petitioner(s) desire(s) to have her name(s) changed from Fiona Irene Brigstocke to: Fiona Irene Brigstocke NGO. Now therefore, it is hereby ordered that all persons interested in the said matter of change of name(s) appear as indicated hereinabove then and there to show cause why the petition for change of name(s) should not be granted.

It is further ordered that a copy of this order be published in the *LA Weekly*, a newspaper of general circulation for the County of Los Angeles, once a week for four (4) successive weeks prior to the date set forth for hearing of said petition.

Dated: Dec. 09, 2002

Murray Gross

Judge/Commissioner of the Superior Court

12/12/02, 12/19/02, 12/26/02, 1/02/03

The court date is 31 January. That's when she officially ceases to be Fiona Irene Brigstocke and becomes Fiona I. B. Ngo.

She's changing her surname from her father's to her mother's maiden name.

That's if she filled in the forms right this time.

The first time she wrote her last name first by mistake. There are a lot of forms. She's doing it all herself using a book called *How to Change Your Name in California*.

Fiona is a 31-year-old historian, teaching at the University of California, Irvine, where she's completing her PhD. She had been thinking about doing this for years.

Both her parents are immigrants; her father British, her mother Vietnamese. With the last name Brigstocke, people assume she's white. She could easily pass for that.

But she doesn't feel British. Or Vietnamese either. If she goes to Little Saigon in Orange County, she never totally feels part of it.

Her Vietnamese, she admits, is not good. In a way, she jokes, as a biracial daughter of immigrants, she's a model American. But that's not a simple identity, either.

At university, she's been studying how Americans see themselves. The dissertation she's working on is all about race, gender and sexuality in Jazz Age New York. She explains it's about how racialization affected what she calls 'narratives of sexuality', and about how – in turn – those narratives were used to build ideas of modern America.

She inherited her love of jazz and blues from her father. One of the performers she's most enjoyed writing about in her dissertation is Gladys Bentley – an energetic, cross-dressing, lesbian nightclub singer who was part of the Harlem Renaissance era. 'It seems,' Bentley once said, 'I was born different.'

Later, in the McCarthy years, she renounced her lesbianism and embraced God.

Fiona is fascinated by the way Bentley rode through what she calls the borderland of these different identities.

Fiona describes herself as 'queer'.

It amuses her that people might assume her name has changed because she's married. Really it's about searching for her own identity through her family's past.

Her mother grew up a Catholic in central Vietnam at the time when the communists were trying to erase memories of French imperialism. The communists killed her two older brothers in the fifties, when Catholics were being persecuted; her mother remembers having to walk to school past the body parts of her brothers' friends.

She grew up negotiating borders too.

Her mother is the only one who has tried to talk Fiona out of the name change. She said Fiona didn't really understand what it meant to be a Ngo.

Fiona says, 'She thought it was important to know exactly how to walk along those borders in order to be safe. By changing my name I'm not walking along the border properly.'

Which is true. It's about the opposite of making herself safe. It's not about rejecting her father's name; it's about what she calls 'racializing' herself.

It made completing those forms quite frightening. 'Racializing yourself in America right now, it's almost like a declaration of war or something, to declare your allegiance with an outsider category.'

But forcing this change on herself excites her. It's a rebirth. In many ways she was raised to be quiet and obedient, a good Asian daughter; oddly, taking on an Asian name is all part of becoming what she calls 'a bad Asian daughter'. Of becoming louder, more disobedient, more self-assertive.

She practises her new signature. She likes the sound Fiona Ngo makes. It has a nice ring to it, a certain alliterative quality. She still faces the tedious process of changing her social security information, her driver's licence, her passport, her bank and credit card information, and her employment records.

Until then, she feels she is inhabiting some peculiar limbo; neither one name, nor the other.

I am a mature well educated tv with an extensive wardrobe and long and varied experience. I am hoping to meet someone with similar interests, either a bi-guy or tv, who is able to accommodate on a regular basis. I would want to establish that there is enough in common to be able to enjoy fun times without hangups before meeting. To leave a voice message, call:

He often remarks how extremely lucky he feels to have been a transvestite. A TV.

When thinking himself into the feminine role, trying to complete the physical transformation, trying to slow his movements to make them more ladylike, something quite profound happens. Something sublime.

Not that he sees himself as born in the wrong body. He is a man who sometimes likes to dress and take on the role of a woman.

Looking back to his earliest childhood there were always little events – rummaging through his mother's underwear drawer and handling her stockings; wearing a silk headscarf. Silly little things.

But it wasn't until he was about 22 and married – with all his new wife's undies to choose from – that it really started. From that he moved on to her skirts and blouses, and the dresses he could squeeze himself into.

Was telling her about it a relief? He supposes it would have been, but it's so long ago now he can't remember.

She has lived with it.

It creates tensions of course. She loves the man, but there is someone else in the relationship too, someone she is in direct competition with; the woman he becomes when he dresses up.

He tries to see it from her point of view. It must be hard for her trying to get close to a husband who is wearing make-up and perfume. But their sex life was never successful, even before she knew about the dressing up.

Sometimes she is OK with it; it depends on her mood. But he can't not do it. It's too important to him. He's tried promising her he'll swear off it. But she knows now that it won't be long before he starts again.

The make-up is always the hardest. Too much is bad. Too little doesn't work, either. Doing her best to be helpful, his wife has offered advice.

Walking in heels takes a little thought before it becomes natural. It's a question of moving more slowly – keeping your knees together and thinking about where you place your feet.

As to buying clothes, he adores it. Though he likes stores like Fenwicks, Austins and Debenhams, it's simpler to buy from catalogues. The choice of sizes is larger. And these days they provide a *very* attractive choice of lingerie.

He has a separate set of drawers for his undies, basques, camisoles and nighties. They lie there, neatly folded; white, dark blue, bottle green, black – even pink. 'I have a photo of myself in pink undies!' he announces proudly.

He gets a particular buzz from calling up the catalogue order lines. Recently he bought two thongs and a bra. He wears a 38C cup, and wanted the woman on the phone to reassure him that it was a full cup rather than a cut-away.

Always very stimulating, that sort of conversation.

And then there are the blouses and skirts. It is his cocktail dresses that give him the most pleasure – though of course if he wants to send out a signal that he's interested in someone, he'll wear a mini skirt.

Apart from his wife, none of his other relatives know. A few female friends. Four of them are women he had affairs with, sleeping together while dressed in negligees.

At the time he had always assumed he was heterosexual.

One of the women asked: 'Do you see yourself man having sex with a woman, or a lesbian having sex with another woman?'

He struggled to answer that. He didn't know.

About fifteen years ago he started visiting a group of fellow transvestites.

That is part of the thrill – to dress in front of others. He dresses at home sometimes, alone, but it's never quite the same.

The only drawback to these gatherings is meeting those men who haven't spent long enough in front of the mirror, or who make no attempt to feminize their mannerisms. He hates that. A badly dressed TV brings out the negative feelings. 'Do *I* look like that?'

It's why he's so picky about his own appearance.

It was at these gatherings that he first started to realize that it wasn't just women who interested him sexually. He found men dressed as women attractive too.

The first man he ever slept with was one of the transvestites who hosted these gatherings. It was incredible. A revelation. He clearly remembers the roughness of Tony's beard under his lips as he kissed him on the mouth for the first time. That's when he started thinking of himself as bisexual. Their relationship lasted four years.

Life changes you. He's surprised how much he's changed over the years, but he's proud that he's done it.

More recently he's started to wonder if he's bisexual at all. He doesn't seem to feel the need for sex with women any more. Maybe it's because it's just so much simpler with a guy. They don't carry the same emotional baggage.

The main problem with life these days is that now he's retired as an IT manager, they've moved to Devon – to the countryside.

In a place like this it's hard to find like-minded men. And, because of his wife, he is unable – as they say – to 'accommodate'. Most other local men are in the same position. It is *very* frustrating.

So he has to find his pleasures where he can. It is Sunday. He is preparing the evening meal for him and his wife dressed in one of his sexy little black dresses. Size sixteen.

It is a moment of stomach-turning happiness. Mouth-watering inner contentment. He feels incredible.

Naturally, he feels like making love too. Just not with the wife he is about to serve dinner to.

6
Clowns

BOBO-THE-CLOWN IS HERE...
Add a cascade of fun to your childrens/party with Bobo-the-Clown & his Magic/Show. 2/hours of fun.

No-hopers and bad jumpers, that's what Arthur Parry used to ride.

Anything with four legs.

If somebody had a horse nobody wanted to get on, they used to phone up Arthur.

Surprisingly he'd get a lot of them round.

He had his successes as a jump jockey, though. Once he came first on Windsor Moon in a three-mile chase at Windsor.

But, as jockeys say, the older you get, the harder you bounce.

He had a few bad falls. Once he was coming into a straight at Hurst Park – it's a housing estate now – on a mare called Copper Rain. She had a bad mouth. It was like trying to steer a lamp-post. When it came to the hurdle she went smack into the wing at the side of it instead. Arthur went right through it and Copper Rain came down on top of him.

He woke up in Epsom District Hospital with a smashed pelvis and a broken ankle. The doctors told him he wouldn't ride for six months.

This was long before the National Hunt Injured Jockey fund had been set up. He had a living to earn, so within six weeks he was back up in the saddle again.

By 1968 he was 37. He'd been lucky. Never had any head injuries. It was a hard life, not being a fashionable jockey, although he'd do it all again. But he had four kids to support, so common sense told him to stop.

For two years he drifted. He worked nights in a plastic extrusion company earning £19 a week; he hated it.

A relative with Down's syndrome was at this clinic. Arthur went along, started mucking about palming coins, making them disappear – simple tricks he'd learned to impress his own kids.

The children loved it so much the staff there asked him to come back.

'I've done everything I know.'

'Just come back and clown about some more.'

'Clown.' It stuck in his head.

He decided to become a children's entertainer.

Gradually he built up an act. He learned quickly not to put on too much make-up. They don't like it.

He bought tricks from Davenports in the Charing Cross Road, or second-hand from other entertainers. His favourite is the old trick Run Rabbit Run, which he bought off a guy who was retiring. The rabbit keeps running between two houses and finally ends up in a top hat a couple of yards away.

Obviously that's another rabbit.

He's 71 now and still in demand. He does two forty-five-minute sets either side of the birthday tea. It's a lot of work.

Children have changed. They're much more hyperactive these days. They stop believing in magic younger.

It can be hard work. He still does the hokey-cokey with the kids. His asthma means he tends to get out of breath. If there are two shows in a single day, he'll come home tired and say to his wife, 'How do you spell "had enough"?'

She keeps asking, 'When are you going to pack it up?'

But it gets him out of the house.

• **Clown clown clown**, one of the funniest number plates around, never fails to get a laugh, £3,500 judit@gerard.

Gerard was 28, skint, working as a State Enrolled Nurse and living at a friend's house in Southport when he heard someone talking about the Austin A70 that some guy had had parked in his garage for twenty-five years.

The numberplate was 'NKB 1'.

Gerard had a thing about number plates. It went back to when he was about 12 or 13, when his dad used to make him look through *Exchange & Mart* to see whether anyone was selling a plate with his initials, JWC.

He thought about 'NKB 1'. It must be worth something.

A year earlier Michael Heseltine had allowed the DVLC at Swansea to start auctioning special number plates and the craze for personalized numbers took off.

'NKB 1' was what dealers call a 'cherished' plate – not one of the numbers auctioned off by Swansea, but one of the desirable pre-1963 registrations.

Gerard had a hunch that it was worth something so he went round there with a friend, knocked on the guy's door and asked, 'Are you interested in selling it?'

'Yes,' said the man. 'Possibly. What are you going to offer me?'

Gerard, who didn't have a penny to his name, suggested fifteen hundred pounds.

'That seems OK,' said the man, cautiously. Then: 'And what about the number plate?'

Gerard offered another two thousand for that: three and a half altogether.

The man hummed and hawed. 'Well, I'm not too sure yet.'

Frustrated, Gerard went to the building society and asked for a loan for £3,500. He had the cheque made out in the man's name and went round and handed it over.

He was now the owner of a clapped-out Austin.

Two weeks later Gerard put a small ad in *The Sunday Times*. He had no idea how much the plate would be worth but he thought he'd start high – twenty-five grand. Halfway through the week he received his first phone call. The man was from Blackburn and his name was Nigel Keith Burrows. NKB. He offered £23,500 for the plate.

Gerard felt his stomach rumble with nerves. Trying to sound calm, he said: 'I'll give you a call at the end of the week.' He wanted to wait and see whether there were any other callers.

For two nights, he couldn't sleep.

Then he phoned Nigel up and said: 'Yeah, it's yours.'

Not long after that the craze died down. The recession kicked in and number plate values crashed, but in the meantime Gerard had just made over twenty thousand in a few days.

He put most of the money down as a deposit for a house; with the rest he went travelling for a year.

First he went to America, heading down to Memphis, hitch-hiking west and then buying an old Buick which took him to California. People couldn't believe he was living off the proceeds of selling a number plate. 'That's absolutely bizarre,' they told him. 'We can buy any number we want to.'

From there he went to China, Malaysia and Hong Kong. He spent three months in Japan and then headed on to Australia.

Back home, he moved into the shed in the garden of the house he'd bought until he'd raised enough from the rent to pay off the mortgage.

His fascination with plates has become an obsession. He spots them everywhere. It's like a reflex.

If he comes across someone at work with a surname of five letters or less he'll start dreaming up plates for them. There are all sorts of tricks. A '5' looks like an S. '12' can read like an R. A '4' can be an A, or if you print it like a digital '4' it could be an L. A '3' looks like an E backwards. And so on.

He follows the news from the DVLA auctions. He'll tell you how 'K1NGS' was the most expensive number plate ever auctioned, fetching £235,000 for the government. He heard a rumour that the Sultan of Brunei bought that one, but he doesn't know whether it's true.

'JUL1E' sold for £85,000, and 'N1GEL' for £69,000.

The government has made somewhere over £500 million out of selling these plates and, he says, they know damn well that they're worth zilch unless people mis-space them. It's illegal, of course. Total government hypocrisy.

His Hungarian wife Judit has picked up the bug for spotting plates. 'I just saw a good one,' she tells him. It's contagious.

It's more of a hobby than a way of making money.

Once unique number plates used to be for ambassadors and millionaires only. Now anyone can have them. He likes that.

He pores over the car number plate bible, *Car Numbers* by Noel Woodall and Brian Heaton. It tries to list as many owners as possible – including the gynaecologist who owns 'PEN15' and 'WOM13'.

On their gold Merc Gerard and Judit have got 'G1JYS', which reads GUYS when the '1' and the J are spaced right. That could be for someone with Guy as their first or last name, or it could be, as Gerard puts it, for someone who plays on the other team.

For a while, when he was working as a registered mental nurse, he had 'C12ASY' on the Merc. The patients used to love it, a mental nurse turning up to work in a car with CRAZY on the number plate. But some of his colleagues in forensic psychiatry thought it was 'unsuitable'.

Right now he has 'K11VGW' on his Honda Goldwing motorbike, which looks a bit like KING W if you push the '1' and the V close to each other.

And on their Jag they've got 'C4OWN' – CLOWN. Gerard bought it a couple of years ago after hearing that 'C1OWN' had sold for twenty-five grand. That made him laugh.

Realizing that 'C4OWN' was still up for grabs, he bought it. It won't be worth that much, but he thought he'd give it a try.

He usually keeps the plates for a few years. He's been driving round with a clown puppet in the back of the Jag for a couple of years. His number plate makes even the most miserable person on earth laugh; he likes that.

But now he wants to sell 'C40WN' because he's

bought 'J10UEG'. Because the U looks like a V it reads J LOVE G.

Judit loves Gerard.

He met her one day when she was over here as a tourist, just walking down the street. He fell in love with her, and when she went home, he hitch-hiked to Hungary to tell her so. They've been married seven years last Valentine's Day; he says they're very much in love still.

Of course, he had wanted to buy 'J10VEG', but that was already owned. By a greengrocer in Covent Garden.

These ten middle-aged guys are getting in his limo now in a pub car park in Hertfordshire, dressed in jeans and leather jackets. Lads' night out. They're all small except for this one huge fellow. He's their boss, taking them out to a club in Hackney.

It's a stretch; a ten-seater Lincoln Town Car. Luke likes it that the people he drives are on a special day out, all having a laugh. There's a bottle of champagne on ice. (Not real champagne – but it's free.) Clean glasses. Luxury interior. Carpets. Lights. Stereo. The hours are long, but because it's weekends, and people are getting married, or partying, it doesn't feel like work at all. Most of the time, anyway. Now and again he knows right away, 'This is going to be bad.'

Even before they start drinking, they're the passengers from hell. Jumping about. Swearing out of the window.

At 1 a.m. he parks outside the club to pick them up as arranged. No sign. Big surprise. He gives them until 1.15 and then starts dialling their mobiles.

Vile language. Really gross.

'If it's another hour I'm going to have to charge you another fifty quid,' he reminds them.

More abuse. 'We 'aven't got no more money.'

But by half one they start to bundle on to the pavement. Literally. They're hammered.

'Oi. We want to stop at a kebab place.'

'I can't do that. You're late already.'

All the way back they're demented. He sees them lighting up and stops the car. It's tricky reminding ten drunken men it's a non-smoking car. Worst is the big guy; he's calling them all names, whacking them, jumping about so much it's making the car bounce.

And when they get close, it's 'Take us all home!'

Luke had been waiting for that. They've only booked a single drop-off.

He sighs. 'If you want that, that's an extra forty quid.'

It's 2.30 a.m. back at the pub where he picked them up. Nobody's getting out. Luke walks up and down outside.

Eventually they all give in. They get out and walk away into the night, shouting more abuse over their shoulders. 'Fuck you.'

All except the boss, still sat in the back.

'I'm not moving,' he says. 'Take me home.'

Luke sighs again. 'Where do you live?'

Broxbourne. As it happens, it's on Luke's way home. With no one left to bully, the big one is quiet now.

And that's when the lights start to go out.

First it's the sidelights. Then the indicators. The stereo goes quiet. All the interior lights go. And he's left driving along in darkness. What is happening? It's like God is messing with him.

And the big guy on his own in the back in the pitch black. He's looking worried now. Maybe thinking Luke is out to get revenge. Going to drive him down a lane somewhere.

But they pull up outside the guy's house. It's massive – looks like it's got about eight bedrooms, and four cars outside.

Of course, the back doors to the limo won't open. They're supposed to when the car stops, but the electrics have gone, completely. It's the alternator, but the guy doesn't know that. He's paranoid, darting from one side to another, struggling with each door.

Luke is wondering how on earth he's going to get him out when all of a sudden he sees the car bouncing. The guy is hurtling right down the middle. He takes a dive at the small partition behind the driver's seat. Somehow, head first, he tumbles through, flies over the driver's seat and winds up on his arse on the pavement.

He gets up and smiles goofily. 'Here,' he says.

He's holding out a £25 tip. Amazing.

And Luke drives the rest of the way home in total blackness.

They're not all like that, though.

7

First thing she said was, 'That's going'

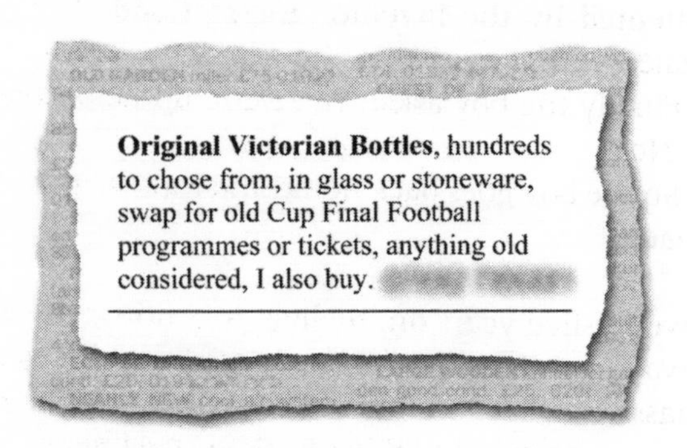
Original Victorian Bottles, hundreds to chose from, in glass or stoneware, swap for old Cup Final Football programmes or tickets, anything old considered, I also buy.

A 15-year-old boy in a field spots something.

A dark shape flying up into the air and falling back to earth, over and over again.

As he walks closer he realizes that what he's seeing is earth, flying up into the air and falling on a mound of soil – about four feet high and growing.

At first the boy thinks it must be an animal digging. But what sort of animal could be that big? Curious, he approaches and sees the soil glittering in the sunshine.

Closer to, he sees what it is that's shining – pieces of broken glass and pottery.

Below ground a man is digging. This is the 1970s, when bottle collecting is a new craze. The boy has never heard of it. For two hours he watches, fascinated. The man carefully unearths an unbroken Codd bottle – one of the Victorian fizzy-drink bottles patented by the inventor Hiram Codd. The bottle is sealed with a marble in the neck.

Finally the boy asks: 'You mind if I get a spade?'

'No.'

So the boy goes back home and returns with his own spade.

Twenty-five years on, he lives in a house a few streets away from Blackpool Tower which he shares with his massive collection. Two attic rooms are filled, plus a garage crammed with unwashed specimens.

They're everywhere. His favourites are the ones with the word 'Blackpool' on them. Every real collector has his own speciality. You have to, otherwise you'd be overwhelmed.

For fifteen years he dug up disused refuse sites around Blackpool. You get to know the signs: elderberry bushes or clumps of nettles growing on uneven ground. He used to look through old OS maps for clues, maybe where a farmer had filled in a pond.

Once he found a sock containing the foot bones of a 15-year-old girl, dismembered by her murderer about twenty years before. The rest of the body had been found by other bottlers a few years earlier.

He had mixed feelings about the dead girl. He felt sorry for her, but was also upset that he and four other bottlers had had to abandon the 18-foot hole they'd dug just when they were getting to the good stuff.

Then, ten years ago, he did his back in.

It might have been the digging, but he prefers to blame twelve years working in paint shops, bending down to spray cars. Now he's awake all hours at night with the pain.

He can't dig any more. He has tried collecting everything – war medals, coins, matchboxes, beer mats, Cup Final tickets and programmes. He tried metal detecting. Too many ring-pulls. Dumped that idea as a load of codswallop – a word he'll tell you derives from Mr Codd's patented bottle. But his new passion never lasts. It always comes back to bottles.

His wife left him too, partly over the bottles, which filled every surface of the house. In the end he had to sell some to pay her off, which was a bit of a heartbreaker.

He even sold his gas cooker first to put off selling his treasures.

It's a permanent struggle now, to keep his collection intact. He doesn't mind getting rid of the rubbish, but selling the rarities breaks his heart. He raises money buying and selling oddments he finds at boot sales or in *Loot*.

The other day a hit-and-run truck driver wrote off his car. He only had third-party insurance, so he had to sell a Warner's Safe Cure bottle in rare aqua-coloured glass to an American collector. He paid £1,815 for it.

He hates selling them, though.

The collection is like his diary. He'll look at a bottle and think: This one was about half three in the afternoon on a sunny day, about eight foot down in the hole. I remember shouting to my mate John, 'Look at this!'...

Even the humblest HP sauce bottle gets him thinking about who might have emptied it before they threw it away. 'Daft as it sounds,' he says, 'there's a million and one stories behind every bottle...'

• STAR WARS R2-D2 full size. This has taken 3 years to make. Offers in the region of £1,000.

R2-D2 was built in the back room of Geoff's dad's shop – the Bexhill Pet Centre.

His body is made mostly out of wood. The feet are worked by windscreen-wiper motors and the head is made from a Space Hopper, some papier mâché, some car body filler and all that sort of shit.

It was Tom's idea. Geoff's not even that much of a *Star Wars* fan.

Geoff agreed to help build it just to shut him up.

Tom has been into *Star Wars* since he saw the first movie at 7 years old. Everyone was. He's 32 now and has a massive collection of *Star Wars* merchandise. Anything from huge cinema displays right down to *Star Wars* crisp packets.

He's proudest of the original action figures, still 'carded' – meaning they're still wired to the original packaging. He even owns some of the genuine panels from Queen Amidala's spaceship.

A mate once tipped him off that they were breaking up the set for *Star Wars Episode One* and you could buy bits of it from a scrapyard near the M25. Tom went off to the scrap dealer and came back with 2 tons of tail fin from one of the submarines in *The Phantom Menace*. It was 15 feet long and he had to hire a lorry to deliver it to his car bodywork shop.

The shitter was that when he had to move out of those premises two years ago, he couldn't get anyone to shift it.

In the end Tom had to abandon it, and the tail fin was demolished along with his old workshop to make way for new houses.

Only cost him thirty quid, though.

And it was, he admits, kind of shit. But when he watches the DVD of *Phantom Menace* he can just make it out. 'Look,' he shouts. 'There it is!'

Tom had always fancied an R2-D2. Eight years back someone had offered him one of the originals from *The Empire Strikes Back*. They wanted £10,000, though, and even if he'd scraped his last pennies together and mortgaged the cat he could only have raised half.

So he decided to build his own. He never expected it to take so long.

Three years of pissing around at the back of Geoff's dad's shop. Sanding it. Spraying it. Doing all the intricate stuff.

During those three years, his whole life changed. Two years ago Tom set up his own business, Bexhill Auto Body. Being in that business was good when it came to painting R2-D2, but it hasn't left him much time for the robot.

The whole thing dragged on. It became an utter, utter pain in the arse, to be honest. And yet he definitely wanted a full-size R2-D2.

When Geoff's dad left the Bexhill Pet Centre, R2-D2 followed Tom to his car body shop, and sat in the office. One customer spotted him and insisted on helping with the detailing.

It's a bloke thing. At the end of the day, blokes don't want to grow up. They all want to be Peter Pan. They want to carry on living their childhood. That was the only time they didn't have to get up for work and answer to the taxman – and all that crap.

There's been another change in Tom's life, too. In January he and his girlfriend were married in Vegas.

His wife isn't interested in *Star Wars*. She doesn't even watch the films.

He doesn't think she minds his interest.

True, she did used to get a little pissed off with him

when his one-bedroom flat was just crammed full of the boxes that house his collection. Let's put it this way – when you have a dressing table you really want to see a mirror, don't you? Not just boxes full of Scoutwalkers.

For a while Geoff stashed some of the collection in his attic, and Tom's mum kept some in her loft – until she discovered she had mice up there.

But now Tom and his new wife are buying a house together in Bexhill. Tom wants the money to do the place up. He's put the whole collection up for sale.

R2-D2 too. Tom'll be sad to see it go. It's like Peter Pan growing up.

Next week he's still taking the day off, though. It's the preview of *Episode II – the Attack of the Clones*.

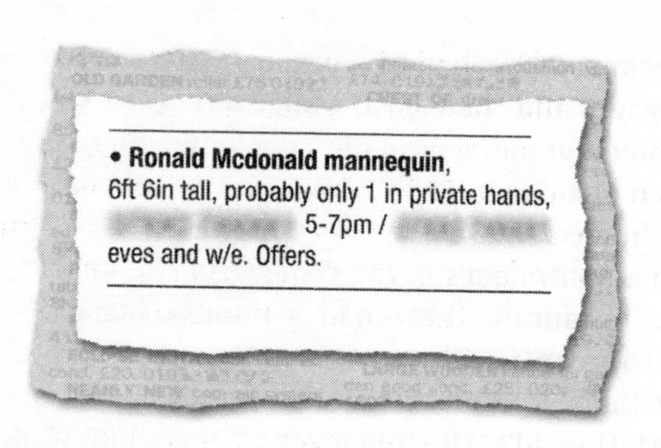

• **Ronald Mcdonald mannequin,**
6ft 6in tall, probably only 1 in private hands,
5-7pm /
eves and w/e. Offers.

Things were going well.

Dave was in building design services.

He'd begun by doing up buildings for Yates Wine Lodges. Then he did up pubs for Boddingtons, and then for Wilson's breweries.

After that he started working as a contractor for a company that installed and maintained all the interiors for McDonald's in the north of England and Scotland. It was a small business. Colin the boss treated him like one of the family.

It meant a lot of driving, anywhere from Stoke up to Glasgow. If they were inundated in the south he'd go down there and give them a hand too. But everything was great. The money was absolutely brilliant. Each move had been upwards. By the time he was with McDonald's he was on £15 an hour – which was money all them years ago – working a hundred hours a week, *and* he had six weeks' holiday. He had a mortgage and had just bought a 4x4 Sierra for seventeen grand.

Then one day in 1991 it all stopped. He'd been away from home about two weeks working when he turned up to a McDonald's in the Gateshead shopping mall.

The restaurant there had a brand-new boss Dave didn't recognize. The new man was saying he didn't want Dave working on his restaurant. So he phoned the McDonald's area manager to find out what was going on.

'It's not one of ours any more,' the man said.

'*What?*'

Dave phoned his gaffer Colin. Colin too was frantically attempting to figure out what was going on, trying desperately to get through to the chairman of McDonald's. He wasn't getting anywhere. Most of the people that he usually dealt with were no longer at their desks. Overnight, the UK company had just sold off most of its stores to individual franchises. And the franchises no longer required Colin's services.

Overnight, the company Dave worked for was bankrupt. Colin lost everything. He still owed a hundred grand to his own suppliers, but there was no money coming in any more. Dave too was owed, around five and a half grand.

It was the end of the world.

Dave didn't want to put in invoices for what he was owed. 'Go on,' said Colin. 'The government will pay you so much in the pound.'

'Yeah, but it's coming off you, isn't it?' said Dave. 'Whatever they pay me they're going to come back to you for.'

So before the receivers arrived to close up the place, Colin called Dave and told him to come to his unit on the trading estate in Ashton. 'Take what you want,' he said.

Dave was like a magpie, taking this and that. He took the kids' mirrors and the McDonald's prints. He took loads of the McDonald's all-in-one table sets, with the two tables and four chairs. He gave them to all his friends. For years afterwards they kept them in their gardens – until the Formica peeled.

The Ronald McDonald was standing in the unit, almost seven foot tall, with the one big hand in the air, waving.

It was a fluke it was there. It had just come back from being re-resined. Dave loaded it on to a flat-back trailer and drove it home. Ronald lay there, smiling, arm raised.

Dave remembers how, on the way home, two coppers in a police van came up behind him. Dave was wondering whether they were going to ask him what he was doing with it, but all they did was wave back at Ronald.

He hauled it round into the back garden, stood it up there, then said to the missus, 'I've got a garden gnome.'

She walked into the kitchen and saw smiling Ronald McDonald for the first time through the window. She screamed. First thing she said was, 'That's going.'

Twelve years later it's still there.

She is too, though for a while it looked like she wouldn't be.

Picking Ronald up made Dave feel better. But not for long.

He'd never been laid off before. It hurt. It really hurt. From a thousand a week, Dave was down to £65. He got nothing else because he'd been self-employed – just social security. With two kids to support, they fought to keep the new house, cutting back on holidays and anything else they could, but everything else was repossessed. These were the days of super-high interest rates. It was a proper nightmare.

For a year he was in shock. He had a breakdown. He couldn't even get out of the chair. He had to see a psychologist. The missus found it hard; they separated for a while, but managed to get through it.

It took years to pick himself up, gradually finding bits and pieces of work. After Colin went bankrupt on him, Dave felt he had to be self-employed. For about eight years he wouldn't work for anyone else in case it happened again. He's never had a credit card since, for fear of getting into debt. It's safer that way.

All through it, Ronald stood in the garden, smiling, waving. He's a feature.

And he has his uses too. They live in a part of Manchester where there's a lot of burglary. They were robbed twice just before Ronald arrived. Dave put a garden light on him that turns on automatically. Occasionally you see it come on, and hear someone scrambling back over the wall. They've not been burgled in eleven years.

One man offered to buy it once, unprompted; he offered Dave a car and £500 in cash. He wanted to place it halfway across a shared driveway just to piss off a pompous neighbour.

Another night Dave was sitting around having a drink with a few mates when they came across this advertisement saying, 'McDonald's memorabilia wanted'. One mate sent off an email for a laugh and minutes later the reply arrived: 'What have you got?'

The advertiser called up on the phone. It turned out he was a McDonald's fanatic. He'd decorated his living room like the inside of a McDonald's, with the tables and chairs, a counter and even the little drinks dispensers. A real Ronald McDonald would be the pièce de résistance. 'Name your price,' he said. He was offering to give over a thousand for it.

A few hours later the McDonald's fan's wife called up, begging Dave not to sell it to her husband. 'It'll mean divorce,' she pleaded.

Dave kept it.

His own wife warmed to it in the end. She planted a tree between it and the house, so you couldn't see it from the kitchen any more.

Their two older kids loved to play on it. When their eldest was five he used it as a climbing frame, hanging all over it. He used to bring all his friends round to show them Ronald McDonald in the garden. That was when his wife began to thaw.

But their youngest has started saying he's frightened of Ronald. He doesn't like the smile. Sometimes Ronald chases him in his sleep. They've covered over the Ronald McDonald mirror in his bedroom with a cloth. Ronald McDonald has to go.

For the moment he's still there in the garden. There's a little moss on him, but that will wash off.

There's a man from London coming up at the weekend. A dealer. Pretending to be ignorant. 'What does a – ah – Ronald look like?'

'They must think we all eat tripe and onions still,' says Dave.

Dave is going to miss Ronald. He's been part of the family.

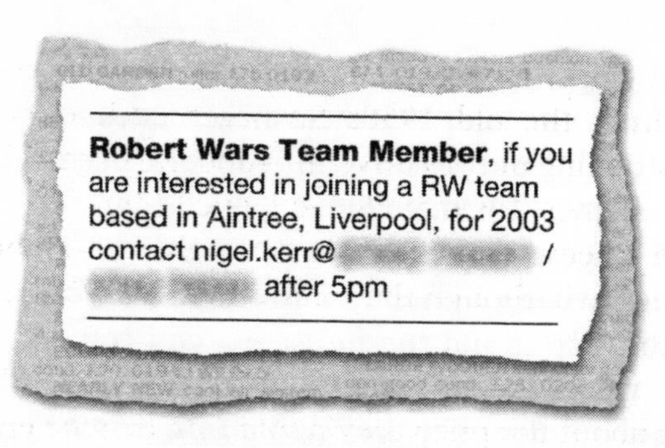

Nigel has been advertising for partners in his *Robot Wars* team for ages. He's put adverts in shop windows, and cards in Asda. He's been to battle shows to display his machines, hoping to find like-minded enthusiasts. No one's come forward.

He thinks it's Liverpool. No one there is interested.

There used to be one other *Robot Wars* fan in Liverpool, but he's gone to live in America because he thinks the show is much better over there.

And anyone who does express an interest in helping him quickly changed their mind when they see how much work it is just lifting 16 stone of robot into the back of a van.

Back in 1994 he was watching *Tomorrow's World* when they showed the new American craze for robot fighting. When he saw it had come to the UK he started on his own wedge-shaped 40-kilogram machine, Hard Cheese.

Nigel works for BT, so he was able to salvage some parts from the old 1950s Strowger exchanges they were stripping out. To drive the robot he used old Ford wiper engines. His mate Steve helped him.

Hard Cheese won the middleweight championship on series two, though they showed only six seconds of it on the TV.

Five weeks later Nigel phoned up the producers asking about the prize they'd told him he'd be getting.

'Oh. We sent it to you. Didn't you get it?'

They said it was lost in the post, so they'd have another made. When it arrived it was a piece of metal mounted cock-eyed on a piece of wood. After that Steve lost interest.

'There's no point,' he said.

Hard Cheese was beaten in series three, but by then Nigel was already building Viper01, the Virtually Indestructible Precision Engineered Robot, a more sophisticated heavyweight machine.

He builds them in his garage. Space is tight so some of the equipment ends up in the house he lives in with his mother. Last winter, after his batteries split in the frost, he started keeping them in his bedroom.

Viper01 was entered for an untelevised trial fight in series five. Halfway through the fight he fried some circuits trying to escape his opponents. Realizing the robot wouldn't go forwards, Nigel hid the damage by only driving backwards for the rest of the fight. Even crippled, Viper01 still won.

That Friday, just before Nigel was about to leave work, the producers called. 'You're in the show. Be here Monday morning.'

That Saturday it rained all day. Unable to find anyone to help unload it, Nigel worked on Viper01 in the back of his van, tailgate up in the downpour. He reduced the power to the transistors but it was pure guesswork. He couldn't get Viper01 out to test it.

He discovered his mistake in the battle arena. Viper barely crawled and was easily beaten. All they showed was a shot of Viper whirring motionlessly.

After that Nigel vowed he wouldn't bother entering again unless he found someone to help him. Too much effort.

He's still advertising. Now he picks up a copy of *Loot* to look in the personal ads section for his latest attempt.

He reads the misprint. '*Robert* Wars? Typical.'

8
Under the skin

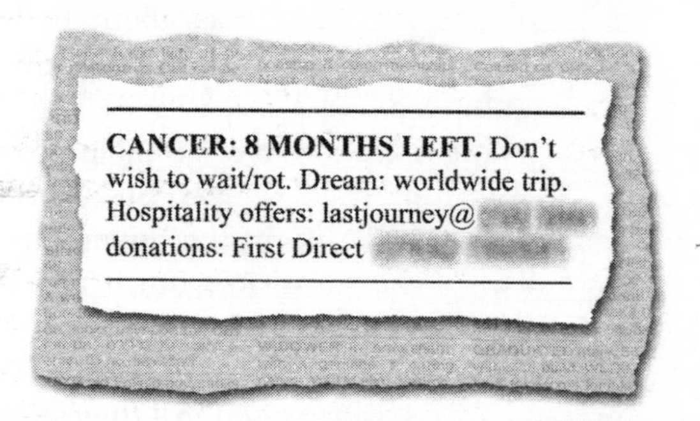

CANCER: 8 MONTHS LEFT. Don't wish to wait/rot. Dream: worldwide trip. Hospitality offers: lastjourney@ donations: First Direct

In Toronto the weather is beautiful – an Indian summer.

He's here for the film festival. He sits in his hotel room before going out to see more movies.

Someone who answered the advert said: 'Look, I'm in Toronto for a conference. There's always a spare bed in the hotel room. Why don't you come and stay? It doesn't cost me anything.'

From here he'll hire a 4x4 and head through South America on the Pan-American Highway. He reckons he has a couple of months before sickness curtails more strenuous activity.

Then to Australia and New Zealand and finally Asia.

In Tibet he plans a little time for spiritual reflection before he dies there. He hopes no friends or relatives attempt to find him. They have no way of contacting him other than his email address; he has made it difficult for them even if they want to.

A few months ago he'd been about to take a job in Europe working for a big American corporation. Badly in debt after completing his MBA, he needed the job and was lucky to get it.

They required a full health check. He remembers joking with his friends about what they'd find. He was 33 and didn't imagine anything could be wrong. First there was a drugs test; then an HIV test.

When the doctor called him into his office he knew it was bad news. He'd travelled a lot; maybe it was malaria. When he discovered he had only months to live, he was numb, shocked. He had advanced small-cell lung cancer.

A great job in a beautiful city in Europe; he had to put all that aside. Already in debt, he faced a decline into further financial dependency. News trickled through to friends and relatives.

They'd say they were sorry, but he could see in their faces that they didn't know how to deal with his situation. Sooner or later, he felt, as he went through the chemo and the radiotherapy, they'd start avoiding him.

He thought, This is going nowhere.

Great ideas always come at sunrise, he thinks. One night he went out drinking in London with some friends, and after that they continued the party back at home. Alcohol had removed inhibitions, and he started taunting his friends, 'What would you do in my place?'

They told him they'd do all the things they'd always wanted to do without caring about the consequences. He couldn't imagine himself acting in that way.

But the more he thought about it, the more he realized they were right.

While he was still in good health he would say goodbye to his friends and his family and embark on a really, really wonderful journey. That way they wouldn't have to go through the pain of seeing him wither away. And he felt suddenly liberated.

'Great,' said his friends, suddenly serious. 'But what about the money?'

How he acquired the money is the reason why he doesn't want to give his name. He worked in the financial services industry, so he knew how much he could raise by extending his overdraft, by asking for loans for work on his house, by pushing his credit card limits.

He doesn't feel 100 per cent good about taking money that isn't his – but there is a right time to be selfish.

Of course, there are still the repayments – and the countries that don't take credit cards. That's partly why he put the advert in.

It turns out that very few people who write to him are offering money. Mostly they offer him accommodation. The ad must have made it out of *Private Eye* on to the Internet, because now he's receiving eight to ten offers a day.

Now he travels, meeting them; they are all really great people. Many, he discovers, have lost a relative or friend to cancer themselves.

When he leaves, he tries to ask them for a little financial contribution to his journey – something he would never have dreamed of doing when he was healthy. But usually they become emotional in their goodbyes, and then he finds it impossible to ask.

Last week he was in the American deserts in Utah, Arizona and California. He watched the sunrise slowly filling up the wilderness around the Grand Canyon. In Death Valley he marvelled at how life persisted there. He finds a beauty in the way that nature carries on; it doesn't really care about him or his predicament.

He tries to avoid any grand thoughts, though. Right now he's trying to enjoy the moment.

• Iraqi soldier's diary. Captured – Desert Storm. e-Bay item #

At the beginning, it was scary. The first Scud Iraq launched into Saudi Arabia in January 1991 landed about a mile from Khobar Towers, where Dave and his transportation company were billeted.

They put on their chemical suits and waited for six hours, not knowing what was going to happen.

But by the time 1486 Company were ordered to assemble in Kuwait close to the Iraqi border, the ceasefire had been signed. The war was over.

There a colonel briefed them. 'This,' he said, 'is the mother of all convoys.' The largest single convoy the US military have assembled in any war.

They set out on hastily built roads through the desert, Dave's 14-ton semi leading the company's trucks. It was an exhausting drive over a rough, bumpy landscape.

They drove for two days straight. On the second day, they reached the road to Basra. They hadn't yet cleared the vehicles that littered the road – the convoy had to weave in and out of them. There were the bodies, too.

On the return journey, Dave ran over one by mistake. Just half a body, really, from the waist downwards. That took him by surprise.

Today, working as a policeman at a juvenile detention centre in Richmond County, Ohio, he sometimes wonders whether that actually happened.

Their destination turned out to be a front line captured by marines. It was a strange place. Everywhere there were abandoned tanks, artillery, anti-aircraft guns and weapons. There were massive piles of rifles.

Their job, they were finally told, was to load up the abandoned tanks and take them back to the safe zone.

They were there four or five days in more than 100 degrees of heat. Dave had only one set of clothes. Around them they could hear the explosions of other weapons being destroyed.

The foxhole was close by. That's where he found the diary: an A4 hardback notebook covered in Christmas wrapping paper.

Dave couldn't understand the writing, but there were drawings, too, in pencil and crayons. Whoever had drawn them was a really good artist. There was a portrait of a moustached man. Another of an eagle, its chest pierced by an arrow and a curved sword. And the one he was most struck by – a strange picture of a woman's face, overlapped by a cat's face, and half a small bird.

Back in Khobar Towers, Dave befriended a Saudi soldier and persuaded him to read the diary and tell him what the entries said.

The Saudi read fragments. The writer was a conscript. Dave never discovered his name, but he wrote that Saddam had told him to go to Kuwait and kill Kuwaitis. His family cried as he left. The troops were so badly under-equipped that the diarist rode to Kuwait on the back of a donkey.

He writes about how there is so little food they lick their plates clean after eating. He misses his girlfriend. He is sick. He doesn't want to fight. He is afraid he will die.

Dave doesn't know whether he did die. Maybe he was captured. This guy had no choice: fight for Saddam or be killed.

The experience made Dave love his own country even more than before. And now it's all happening again. Dave follows the news closely. He watches Fox News because CNN is too slanted; you hear too many left-wing voices on it.

The world's a scarier place than it used to be. He sits and watches and thinks Iraq is going to get pretty bloody. And it's going to get worse. Anything can happen. Afghanistan. Iran. North Korea. There could even be a world war.

Sometimes he feels bad about the diary. There's an address in the back. He should have sent it to the soldier's family. But it's in Arabic, and Dave can't read it.

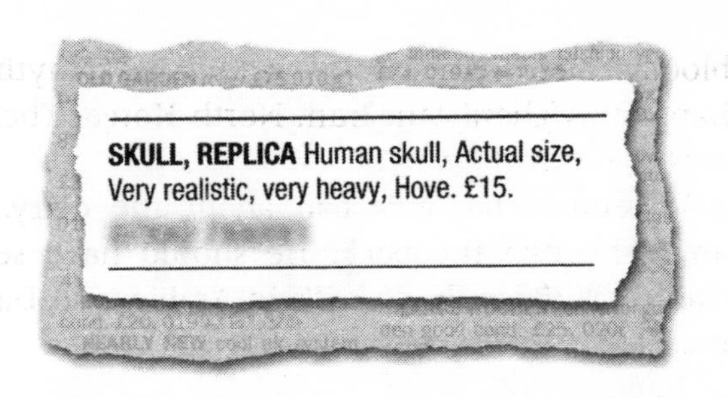
SKULL, REPLICA Human skull, Actual size, Very realistic, very heavy, Hove. £15.

Tuesday night is alternative night at the Gloucester in Brighton. Goth, indie, hard rock. John likes hard-core noisy stuff – early Killing Joke, Norma Jean, Circle of Dead Children… At the last minute, he decides to go.

There's a Canadian girl there. She's on holiday, visiting the UK on a cheap air ticket, just having a little fun. Their eyes meet across the dance floor. It's hard to miss John. At 34, he has long hair falling down his back. They talk. They arrange a date for the next night. They fall in love.

All the rest of the winter they call each other up once or twice a week, clocking up huge phone bills.

In February she comes back and they marry. And it's good. They have that Libra/Aquarian thing going on. She likes Led Zeppelin and Loreena McKennitt – nothing as noisy as John's tastes. She likes beautiful things – appearances are important to her. He says he likes what's going on underneath the surface. Under the skin. Like the skull.

A friend of his wife's gave it to John. 'He likes Gothy kind of things, doesn't he? I don't want it. It gives me the creeps.'

It gives his wife the creeps too.

He thinks it's quite nice. He puts it in a corner with a couple of candles near it. Visitors look and say: 'Uh, that's... nice.'

She hadn't planned on going back to Canada. She likes it here: Toronto is ugly, she says.

But when her brother's cancer returned a month ago she flew back. She didn't want to be over here if he died. They don't know how long he's going to last. He's hanging on in there.

John was born in Brighton. He's 38 now. His life was going nowhere, doing contract office cleaning. Now he's suddenly realized that everything can change.

Knowing that she might be out there for some time, she said, 'Let's both go over there. You liked it when you visited.'

Prompted by his brother-in-law's illness, he's decided to follow his wife to Canada – permanently.

It's surprised him. He thought he was the sort of person who never liked change; now he sees he was just the sort of person who thought that this was as good as it would get.

Now his life is full of possibilities. New places. New music. New friends – like Ambrose, his wife's best mate. He's gay. John has never had a gay friend in his life up until now.

'You're sure about this?' his old friends ask, anxiously.

'Yeah,' says John.

'Wow,' they say, shocked. 'You're selling everything. I mean, you've had that guitar since you were 22!'

'Yeah. And now it's knackered.' So what?

They say, 'You won't start saying "dude" and stuff like that?'

'I already do!'

Cheer up, you miserable bastards. Live a little. Hopefully he can do a little better than be a contract cleaner out there.

OK, it's going to be strange. His wife's parents are giving them a small house on 11 acres of land, north of Toronto in the middle of nowhere. There's a barn which she's thinking of converting into stables so she can keep horses.

Here in Brighton, he lives in a crowded city. If he wants a pint of milk he just nips across the road. There he'll have to drive for twenty minutes.

He's used to city lights. It'll be pitch black there at night.

There he'll have his own creek in the back yard, with wild geese in it. Wow, thinks the city boy. That's my creek.

Maybe he'll get a dog. He could walk 100 yards and it would still be his garden. He practises saying, 'Get off my land!'

His wife says there are sometimes deer too.

She phones him up. Fifteen inches of snow fell there this morning. You can't see any other houses. There aren't any. At night it's so dark she's finding it hard to be on her own. She can't sleep.

'Will you hurry up?' she begs him.

He's itching to be there. He's pretty much sold up everything now – apart from the skull. He's sold his guitars for a couple of hundred each. His Roland eight-track has gone, which he was quite gutted about because they've discontinued it now. There's a 56k modem he paid £90 for that no one wants. All the debris of his former life. He doesn't want any of it. Any day now, he'll buy the ticket.

It's amazing how much things can change. It's not just the guitars he's leaving behind. People pick fights with him because of his long hair. They stare at it. Or at least, he feels they do. In Canada he steps off the plane and he doesn't feel anyone even cares about that.

That's the funny thing. They're probably not even staring at him in Brighton any more. But he feels they are. He realizes it's all sorts of baggage he's leaving behind.

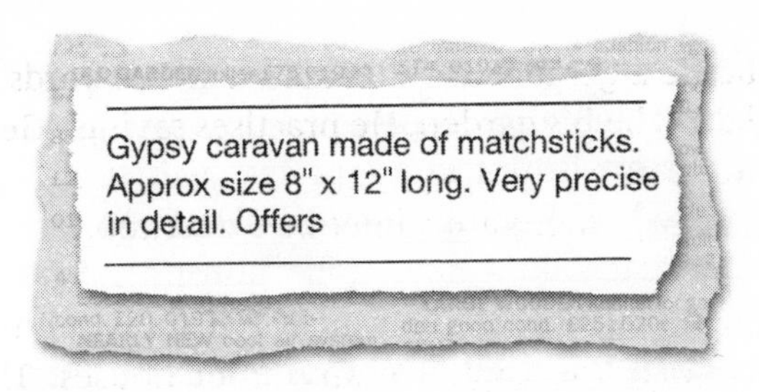
Gypsy caravan made of matchsticks. Approx size 8" x 12" long. Very precise in detail. Offers

Terry dreams about getting on *Who Wants to Be a Millionaire.*

He doesn't think he's supersonic bright, but he's got a lot of common sense. He was watching it the other day and he got all the questions right except one. The big one was which of the following is a round fish? A) a cod; B) a flounder; C) a plaice; or D) a hake.

Terry knows for a fact it's a cod.

He should do. He was a match angler. All the competitions. One of the top ten on the Isle of Sheppey. There have been times when he's scratched around for 50p here and there for the £5 entrance fee, gone in and – whack! – cleared up and come away with fifty quid.

He was asked to fish for England but refused because they told him he had to buy his own blazer and grey flannels.

'Bollocks,' Terry told them.

Terry's disabled. He fell down a bloody sea wall fishing. It hurt like hell but he wasn't going to give up because he'd paid his thirty-five-quid competition fee; so the other anglers propped him up on a box and he carried on fishing. Caught five fish too. He was really pissed off because he missed a £100 prize by a whisker. That would have done him fine, a hundred quid.

Afterwards it turned out he'd broken his back.

That was four years ago.

He still fishes, though.

He's has already had two rollickings about the ad. One from Shirley, his eldest, the other from his missus, Helen. They don't think it's right to sell it. Really, it's the sort of thing that should be left in the family.

But they're brassic.

Broke.

They need a few bob.

It's exquisite, says Terry. Wheels, shafts, everything, all made out of matchsticks. Painted green with flowers on. And inside it's all decorated. Stuff on the floor and everything. And if you look through the windows the other thing you'll see inside is the name Kizzy. She was only tiny when Terry's brother – Kizzy's dad – Shane made it. She's grown up now. An absolutely gorgeously stunning girl.

Terry never thought Shane would have had the patience to do anything like that.

Shane made it when he was inside. Maidstone or Elmlea, Terry can't remember. It was so long ago. And Shane spent a lot of time inside. A little sod, says Terry. Loved him to death, but he was always a little git. Never hurt anybody, but, yes, he was a crook.

Burglary; cars. He'd nick a different one every evening, take a girlfriend out then creep back at three in the morning and lock it up again so that in the morning the bloke would come out and say, 'I never left it there!'

A mischievous little sod, his younger brother Shane.

For a while Shane had lived on a farm in Leicester with this right slag of a woman. Right fat and horrible, she was. Terry never knew what he saw in her. But it was good for him up there. He was an outdoor man. Loved a bit of poaching. He could take the pheasants out no problem with the farmer not 200 yards away. It was like he was half pikey, not that it's in the blood. But they got into some aggro up in Leicester and so they moved down to Cornwall, right near the Lizard.

They lived there until he and the slag had this big row. She chucked some of his gear out of the window. Of course, he got the hump and said, 'I'll punch you in the bloody eye in a minute.'

Not that Shane would have, Terry says. He was a hard boy, but soft inside.

But she got the police round. 'He's threatening to beat me up. To kill me.'

The police said to Shane, 'We don't care where you want to go, but don't come back here.'

He didn't even have the money for the train. So he called up Terry and Terry had to find it somewhere, not that he had any either. He had to call up the train people and say, 'I'll pay you when he gets here.' It took some explaining.

So Shane got on the train and Terry went up to Paddington to meet him. Two o'clock in the morning, waiting for him to arrive. Got tapped up by some bloke. Almost filled him in there on the platform. Fell asleep. Woke up bloody freezing.

The train comes in at five. All the passengers go by. 'Fucking hell. He's missed it.'

So Terry walks along the train just to make sure and there he is, curled up on the seat asleep. He'd got one suitcase and a fishing rod with him. Terry shook him. 'Come on, son. We're here now.'

He'd been away from Sheppey a while, but he was home now. That was the Monday. Three years ago now.

The following Thursday Terry was at a fishing competition on Deal pier when his mobile rang.

Two blokes in a house on the island overdosed, says his sister, crying her eyes out. One of them is dead.

They say it's Shane. He'd only been home three days. Terry goes mad, crying, trying to pack up, putting his fish in someone else's bucket.

'What's the matter, mate?'

'My brother's been found dead.'

'No. He ain't?'

Terry went to his sister's.

Shane must have been 42.

It was being in prison that got him on to heroin. He didn't used to take it before, when he was on the outside. But he was inside quite a lot. Four years was the longest. Shane knew all the junkies.

He was off heroin when he came back to Sheppey, but he must have fancied a buzz. Boredom? Terry doesn't know.

They said it was stronger stuff than usual. He was overdosed. Someone had injected him in the elbow. Terry could tell you the name of the bloke who did it. The guy admitted it at the coroner's inquest. Terry can't believe that he's still free, walking around Sheerness. The coroner brought back a verdict of accidental death. 'Don't give me that cobblers,' Terry told the man. 'He was killed and you know it.'

Terry thinks they should bring back hanging. Give them a drop of the birch, they won't do it again. Guaranteed.

At the funeral they played that one by Puff Daddy: 'Every Step You Take'. And 'Sailing' by Rod Stewart. Shane had always looked a bit like Rod.

A pest, but Terry knew the real Shane. Underneath, he was a smashing bloke. A smashing, smashing bloke.

Terry and his wife moved from Sheppey after that. The place is going down. You wouldn't believe it.

The missus works shifts as a residential social worker, two nights on, two nights off. She gets paid monthly. They bumble through the first couple of weeks; after that it's a struggle.

But then Helen's little car died; she couldn't get to work without one.

Terry needed to get her a new one, so he had a rake around the garage for things he didn't want. Sold his fishing tackle – the Daiwa Whisker his wife had bought him as a Christmas present. Even his prize Ziplex rod – an original 2500 built by Terry Caroll at Dungeness. An excellent, excellent fishing rod. The Rolls-Royce of rods. Broke his heart. A bloke came round and said, 'I'll take the lot.' Five hundred quid. All gone. Boom.

Got her a little Fiesta with the money. Clean as a whistle. Bargain price. They insured it and there was enough money over to do a proper *proper* shop, like normal families do. Filled up the freezer and stocked up with all the tinned goods, then paid a couple of bills, paid the insurance on the car, and then they're broke again.

But the Fiesta needs taxing soon. That's why he put the ad in to sell Shane's caravan. Shirley says he shouldn't be selling it anyway. Really and truly it's the sort of thing that should be left in the family.

No one has called them up about it, anyway.

PISTOL 7.62 x 25 Tokerave, auto
amo. holster. powerful $195

Raquel wrote poetry. She had a notebook she entitled 'Poetry from the Heart'.

In her small, slanting handwriting she wrote:

My heart is breaking can't you see
Everytime you get mad at me
You call me names you don't really mean
I want to break down and scream.

The 'you' was her husband, Mark, twelve years older than her. She already had one infant daughter, Gabriella, when she and Mark started going out nine years ago. They had met in the town of Corpus Christi, Texas, where they'd both been taking a science class at a local college.

They married in 1997 and had two more children, Santino and Vincenzo, and lived together in Bradenton, Florida, once a quaint plantation town, now a growing city in the flat land by the side of the wide, slow Manatee river.

But Mark was violent. He had had restraining orders placed on him before by his first wife, Estella. They hadn't made any difference to his behaviour. Even after Estella had won the order, Mark would stalk her, dressed in dark clothes. He called her after work; he harassed her friends.

Eventually he was imprisoned for violating the order; even from jail he continued menacing Estella. Every time she heard his voice on the other end of the line she was afraid. He was sentenced to eighteen months for harassing her. He served six.

Estella had three children by Mark. They live with his mother in Bradenton.

When Raquel and Mark met, Mark was also on probation for engaging in organized crime.

Raquel and Mark finally separated last year. Raquel started living with a new boyfriend, Ernesto.

On 19 December she filed for a restraining order against Mark, telling the judge he had abused her physically for nine years. He was threatening her now too. 'Please help me and my children,' she wrote. 'I am deathly afraid of this man.'

Five weeks after Raquel had applied for the restraining order against Mark, she asked the judge to dissolve it so that he could see his children.

The custody battle turned bitter. Both taped their

phone calls to the other to try to gather evidence against their former partners.

At a hearing on 25 April detectives told the court that they believed Raquel was a drug user; they read a transcript of a phone conversation in which she appeared to threaten to kill herself, and maybe also the children, if she lost final custody of them.

So Mark was given temporary custody of the kids. A further hearing was set for the following Monday, 29 April. They were to return to court on 5 May for a divorce hearing; Raquel was planning to marry her boyfriend Ernesto.

On Sunday, 28 April Mark saw the advert in the 'Guns & Rifles' section of the *Sarasota Herald-Tribune.*

He tore out the ad. A Tokarev TT33. A semi-automatic handgun designed by the Soviets in the 1930s, now manufactured cheaply in China and Korea. Its cheapness and availability have made it a popular gun for British criminals too.

Mark's criminal record meant he was barred from buying weapons from gun dealerships under the so-called Brady Law, which requires all dealers to run a criminal background check on any customers and then hold the gun for three days before passing it to the buyer. But private sellers are exempt. This was a private seller. He bought it on a Sunday. Some bullets too.

Around 10.30 p.m. that Sunday night, the bell rang in Raquel and Ernesto's duplex apartment on 12th Street Court East. Raquel opened the door; 9-year-old Gabriella was standing there. Mark had sent her to the door first.

Two-year-old Santino and 1-year-old Vincenzo waited in the car.

Ernesto was in the shower when he heard Raquel shouting, 'Get out! Get out! Get out!' And then shots.

Ernesto ran out. Raquel was lying in a pool of blood outside her bedroom. Gabriella, still in the doorway, was crying. She had seen everything.

Mark was still holding the Tokarev.

Ernesto says he went to check whether Raquel was still breathing, but Mark told him not to touch her. That she was already dead. 'He knew what he was doing and that was that,' says Ernesto.

Mark was still waiting there when the police arrived for him.

Someone covered her with a Winnie the Pooh sheet; Raquel's blood soaked into the cloth. She was 27.

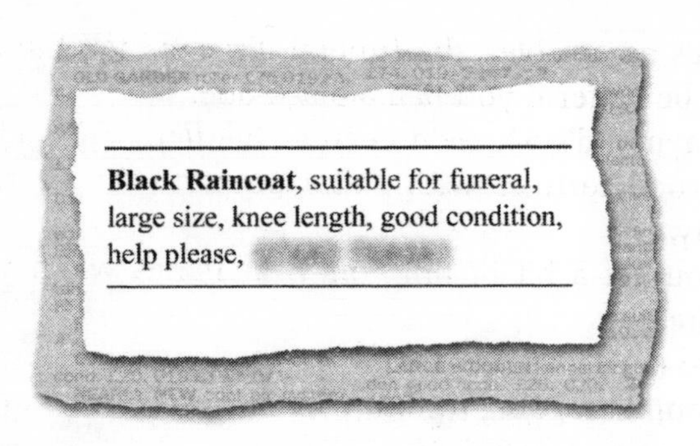

Black Raincoat, suitable for funeral, large size, knee length, good condition, help please,

Raymond has tried all the shops. He wants one just like in the old adverts on the back of the *London Evening Standard* – that guy standing there with a pipe and trilby and a long black mac.

He's rung Burton's, Marks & Spencer and this, that and the other shop but you can't get them any more.

The nearest he could get was one of those posh shops down the West End. They wanted five hundred quid!

The cheapest one was a hundred and fifty. That was in one of those magazines that supply the funeral trade, *Funeral Service Journal*.

He can't afford that. Well, he could, but he's not going to. You only get five quid an hour as a pall-bearer. Twenty quid minimum. That's a lot of coffins you've got to carry just to buy a pall-bearer's raincoat.

He does have a mac but it's grey.

'It's acceptable,' the funeral directors tell him. 'But it'd be better if you had a black one.'

Raymond's 53. He'd been a chauffeur but had a bit of good fortune with some property, so he retired early.

You get a bit of time on your hands when you're retired.

He needed something to get him out of the house – to stop him going round the bend. So he took up pall-bearing two years ago.

The first time he walked into a funeral parlour the dead bodies shocked him. The morticians were still dressing one of them. One look at that and he wanted to run straight out of the room.

But you get used to it. After you've seen ten, fifteen, twenty, you realize you've all got to go some time.

Raymond does about three funerals a week. It's a handy job. 'It suits,' he says.

All sorts do it. The other day he was on with a fireman and a postman. One lad was 21, the other 60.

The average age of the people they're carrying is 70. He buried someone the other day who was 102, but then again he did another one just recently who was only 6 weeks old. At the burial there's the lady who's carried the child for nine months, her beautiful baby, and now she's all fat and ugly because of carrying it and she's lost it.

It's a crying shame. And then they've got to pay for a funeral, on top of it.

Sometimes you get someone screaming and crying. Your job, whatever happens, is not to react at all. So Raymond stands there, head bowed, ready to slip away as quietly as possible afterwards. Disappear into the background.

The cost of it. Cheapest funeral still costs about fourteen hundred quid. When Raymond's own mother and father were buried it was four and five grand respectively. So there's a lot of money in it.

Not for the pall-bearers, though.

Raymond doesn't like to see people spending too much on the funerals he goes to. He'd have a simple one himself. No flowers. After two days the flowers go in a skip and that's it.

A lot of people are buying white doves these days. Ninety quid for the first one, and thirty more for every bird after that. Some families have six, seven, eight. That's £300.

Open the box and up they fly. Gone. Ludicrous.

To the bereaved, it's their loved ones floating up to heaven, he supposes.

Raymond is 6′2″. Bit of a problem.

That means he always stands at the back – which is

the heavy end. The two who are shorter always stand at the front. And because the weight's always on one shoulder it can be a bit iffy. He's known a couple of lads who've gone down with bad backs doing it.

Never dropped one, though. Not yet. Fortunately.

A coffin with a dead body in it is a weight. Unless it's an old, frail person who died of something wasting. Raymond swears that a dead body weighs more than a live one, too. Hence the phrase dead weight.

'If he was 14 stone alive,' he says, 'he'll be 15 stone dead. And then there's the coffin, of course.'

He's doing a job over at Hertford tomorrow. Outdoors. Last week he was standing by a graveside as the Essex rain hammered down. He was wearing a black woollen overcoat that was soaking up the water like it was cotton wool, thinking, Wish I had a mac.

Maybe there's someone who's got fat and can't get into theirs any more. Trouble is, once you've got one, you don't want to let it go.

Lasts you a lifetime, a good mac.

9

Until you got interested in girls

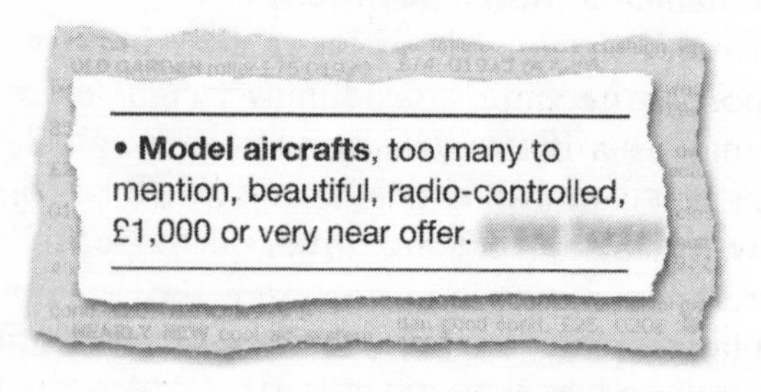

Some people like music, some like football – with Syavosh Ziaei, it was always planes. As long as he can remember he has been fascinated by aircraft. It's the way they just float in the air. It started when he was a boy living in Tehran near the military aerodrome. He would ride his bicycle there to watch the old Wankel-powered planes with the wooden propellers, or American Howards – and later the C-130s.

At 12, he began making his own planes from kits, stretching tissue paper over balsa frames. His first was called a Goblin. That was thirty-six years ago, but he remembers clearly how, even before he had attached the wings, he wound the rubber band and watched proudly as the fuselage shot across the mosaics of his family's patio.

When it was finished, he flew the Goblin near his house, but Tehran's streets are criss-crossed with electricity and telephone wires. The plane ended up snared, dangling from a lamp-post.

Each model he made was better than the last. For two months he imprisoned himself in the house's cellar making a plane called a Sky Scooter, fitting it with his first combustion engine, a Webra 1.5cc motor. He flew it near the military airfield. It flew free. This was pre-radio-control and you never knew where it would land.

As a teenager, he joined the local aviation club – the Royal Flying Club. That was in the days of the Shah. It doesn't exist any more: if it did, it certainly wouldn't be called that. He was a student in the UK when the revolution happened in 1978–9. Because he was already abroad, he stayed. It was simpler than going home.

His friends here call him Sasha.

He married and settled down in London. He worked as a plumber, tiler and kitchen designer, and his wife worked as a medical secretary. It wasn't a happy marriage, though. In his mid-thirties, Sasha started buying and building planes again. He bought his first three-channel radio-controlled plane that summer at the model expo at Sandown Park. It was second-hand and cost about £35, but to Sasha it was beautiful. Other plane enthusiasts showed him how to fly it. Some beginners think it's just like driving a car; but it's a knack that you have to learn.

There was money coming in – he had a good job – and he found himself becoming compulsive about collecting, building and mending planes. There was the Piper PA-20 Pacer he never flew, and the Cessna. They filled up the corridor and the cellar of their home.

His wife never liked the planes. He didn't expect her to go flying with him, but he never expected her to dislike them so much. She pretended she didn't mind them, but underneath she really did. He thinks the planes are the reason why, after about ten years, in 1994, his marriage fell apart. That and his wife's drinking.

It wasn't a good divorce. Neither of them wanted to move out of the place they shared in London, so for more than two years after the divorce they still lived together in the same house.

Things have been hard since the divorce. Sasha became depressed. He says it's like when you fall from a height into water, you go right down and it takes a long time to come back up to the surface. It's only in the past couple of years that he has felt better.

He knows he has too many planes, and he needs the money, because he hasn't worked since the divorce and he wants to go back to visit old friends in Tehran. But he still enjoys building them, modifying them, fitting new engines. And when the weather is good he flies his favourites on the big field between Hammersmith Hospital and Wormwood Scrubs. There are always fellow radio-control enthusiasts down there.

From the moment he's flying his plane, he doesn't think of anything else. He's totally involved with the plane and keeping it in the air. During the worst days of his divorce, it was the only thing that kept him sane, he says.

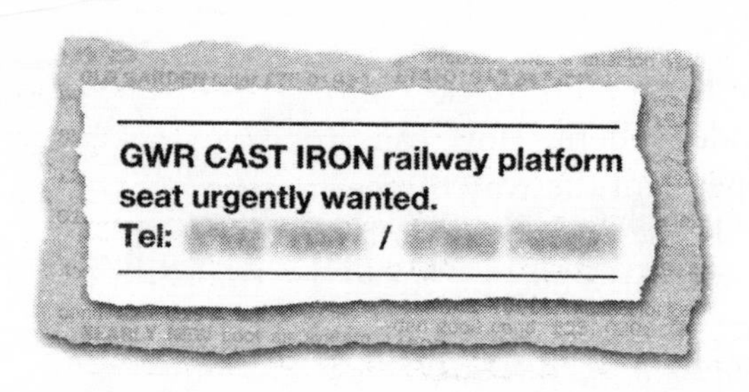

GWR CAST IRON railway platform seat urgently wanted.
Tel:

Robert thinks people who enjoy school are a sad lot.

From the age of 9 onwards he used to bunk off to go trainspotting. He'd be at the end of a platform with a duffel bag and his Tizer and sandwiches, collecting numbers of the locomotives that ran on BR's Western and Southern regions.

A boy could travel wherever he wanted in those days. Robert used to tell his mum and dad that he was going to look round the engine sheds in London, and he'd be off to King's Cross to see if *Mallard* was there. He'd get on a train at Bristol, get off at Paddington, take the Tube round to all the main termini and then go off to see all the engine sheds.

Oh Lord, yes. Kids had more freedom then. Most of your childhood was spent outside. Of course, we're talking the 1950s here. Can you imagine a kid of 11 doing anything like that now?

Sure, there were dodgy people around, just as now. You spotted them. In those days you probably wised up to them a lot quicker, in fact. You learned how to be independent. How can children ever learn to be independent the way things are today?

He'd raise the money for his trips doing paper rounds.

At an early age he mastered three card brag, for money, and that would help pay for the fares.

He'd be gone for days at a time.

At 13 he was buying Rail Rover tickets. For a week he'd have the freedom of the whole Southern Region, travelling round every engine shed from Dover Marine to Padstow. He still remembers each place he went to, right up as far as Doncaster.

He'd sleep in waiting rooms, or aboard the Atlantic Coast Express, waking up to clean his teeth with salt from a BR salt cellar. Sometimes he'd overrun his ticket; it could be eight days before he came home.

OK, so a lot of it was frankly bloody miserable, sitting on windy platforms waiting for a train that didn't show up with no money to buy BR sandwiches.

Or getting chased out of Camden Shed – which is the Roundhouse now – by some fireman who opened up the blower on his engine on him, filling the air with smuts so that you were covered from head to foot by the time you got out.

But.

Thousands of kids did it, gosh yes, swapping stories and tips.

'How do you get into such-and-such an engine shed?'

'Watch it. The foreman there is a miserable bastard.'

It was a hobby until you got interested in girls. And then you'd forget all about trainspotting.

He's 58 now.

Later in life the passion returned. He collects things that remind him of his adventures.

One of the pieces that means most to him is the number plate of a locomotive that used to work between Bath and Bournemouth. He had cadged a ride in the cab.

What you used to do was stand at the end of the platform looking all forlorn until some driver took pity on you.

You'd get niggled as hell if the vicar turned up. Robert doesn't know what it was with steam railways and vicars. They always got a ride. And you'd have to wait.

But this day a driver took him. It happened to be the ace driver of this particular line.

He'll never forget it. Going uphill into a tunnel in the Mendips, the loco was working hard, chucking out sparks. This particular incline was steep. Unable to make headway, the engine slipped to a standstill, still chuffing away.

This was lethal. Sulphurous fumes poisoned the air in the tunnel. Robert was terrified. He thought he was going to die.

The fireman ordered the suffocating boy to lie on the floor, and try to breathe through the gaps in the floorboards, until the driver managed to chuck enough gravel on the line to make the wheels grip again.

In 1968 at an open day at an engine shed in Eastleigh he spotted the number plate of that very loco for sale. Robert watched as the bloke in front of him bought it for fifteen quid. A week's wages. He could never have afforded that.

But he kept his eye out for it. Twenty years later he heard that it had been spotted on this bloke's wall. For two years Robert badgered the man to sell him it. He offered him a colour TV. A video. Even a trip to India. Eventually the guy gave him first refusal.

Now he's added it to his collection of Southern Region and Great Western pieces.

Like the benches. There were four GWR bench designs. Robert has parts of three of them. He's still looking for the complete set.

They're the same ones he used to sit on when he was a little boy, riding steam trains.

10

Something is wrong

Marge and Bill Bent, worked at Madame Tussauds 1977–79. You befriended a young boy called Simon, please get in touch.
If anyone knows Marge or Bill please pass this onto them

Marge and Bill: the 12-year-old boy who used to watch shows at the London Planetarium over and over again during the summer of 1978 wants to say hello. And he wants to say thank you for what you did.

As a young boy, Simon loved light. He still does. Laser shows and light displays make the hairs on his neck stand on end. He's fascinated by the technology, too. The other day he bought himself something that looks like it's from *Doctor Who* – his own X–Y scan laser projector. He also scrounged about £1,500 worth of software to create his own light and music shows at home – a bit like the ones he used to go and see at the Planetarium when he was a boy.

The first time he put on his own show upstairs, all the emotions he'd felt in the 1970s flooded back. That was a few months ago. He's been thinking about Marge and Bill for years. Watching his laser at work was a kick up the backside. That's why he placed the ad.

In 1976 a schoolfriend's mum took him to the new Lasarium show at the Planetarium. Simon couldn't believe what he was seeing. It was fantastic.

Back then, he lived with his parents in a flat in Temple Avenue, off London's Fleet Street. It turned out that his father was having an affair, and at the end of 1977 his parents started living separate lives, although still in the same flat. Some nights his father would be out seeing the other woman. Sometimes he wouldn't come back at all, or came back drunk. His parents would argue. Both of them had children by a previous marriage. Each child took their parent's side. Everyone had an opinion about the split. Torn, Simon felt awful.

The awfulness stretched into the long summer holiday. He was miserable. He wanted to be out of the way. So he escaped to the Planetarium on his own every day. There, he could lose himself in light. It was magical, a break from reality. He was transported somewhere else and would forget what was going on at home.

One day the woman in the ticket office said, 'I keep seeing you around. What's the deal?'

Marge must have been in her early thirties, an ebullient woman with bright red wavy hair. She took him for lunch with her boyfriend Bill, who wore white overalls and worked in the Tussauds maintenance department.

Marge was amazing. All the things Simon couldn't talk about at home, he could tell her. Like how his mother had decided to move out of London, taking him with her. Simon felt he was being uprooted – he didn't even know where to.

Marge and Bill treated him with incredible kindness. They'd say, 'Keep your chin up.' Told him that things would get better.

They just let him get it off his chest. They looked after him. And it helped.

He'd stand by the ticket booth and just talk. When the managers came he had to sneak off, of course. Once, Marge sent him to sit with the woman who operated the Planetarium's Zeiss projector, and she let him work the device for that afternoon's show. Fantastic. That was another reason for not wanting to move out of London.

In 1979 his mother finally took him away, to Milton Keynes. He kicks himself for never having asked for

Marge's number. Maybe he did and lost it.

Against the odds, his parents got back together after a couple of years. Everything worked out. The awfulness went. These days he has a fantastic relationship with his father and mother.

But now, grown up, he realizes that Marge and Bill must have been very special. He's always thinking about them. He'd like to know that they're all right. It's become important to him to tell them that they were right. Everything really did turn out OK.

• **UNFURNISHED STUDIO**, Carlisle Road, white person, NO DSS or Pets, £90 pw, bills extra

Tony Greenstein is appalled.

He's looking at the accommodation-to-let section of the *Friday Ad.*

White person, no DSS.

Tony is the secretary of the Brighton and Hove Unemployed Workers' Centre. He's the veteran of several anti-racist battles.

His first thought is that it's some right-wing crank trying to wind things up, or worse, somebody close to the BNP trying to provoke some argument about free speech. Ex-BNP leader John Tyndall lives in Hove.

He issues an angry press release: 'This is an exclusion clause reminiscent of the 70s proviso in adverts, "No dogs, no blacks, no Irish".'

The advert, he says, is 'blatantly racist'.

Mary is only 56, but she's disabled, with pains in her arms and legs that make it hard for her to walk. The doctors aren't sure what's wrong; she's been going for tests.

She doesn't like to cry, but the other day, when trying to open a tin of beans, she found herself bursting into tears. She doesn't cry much, though. Mostly she takes it in her stride.

She carries a mobile phone with her all the time. She's only had it a couple of years, but it's very handy because she tends to fall over sometimes.

She used to be a nurse, but had to stop working. To ensure an income, she bought a studio flat a couple of years ago.

The girl who's been living there has to move out – she's going to college and can't afford the rent any more. That's why she put the advertisement in.

The calls on Mary's mobile start on Friday morning, when the paper first appears. She is feeling a little poorly, so she ignores them until the afternoon. The first she takes is from a man who says he works in Hove Town Hall. At first he sounds normal. 'Which number is the flat?'

But then he repeats her advert over and over angrily, 'White person. No DSS.'

Mary thinks: He's a nutter. What's he on about? That's not what her advert said at all. She'd read her copy out clearly to the girl at the *Friday Ad*: 'Quiet person. No DSS.'

Something is wrong. Rattled, Mary tries to check the paper, but her disability means she can't make it to the shop that stocks the free magazine.

It's embarrassing sometimes. Some people think she's drunk when they see her trying to stand. She sees them looking at her. Oh my God.

She rings the *Friday Ad*. 'What's it say? I don't have a paper.'

That's when the paper admits there has been a mistake. Lamely, the woman there suggests she unplugs her phone.

Mary says, 'That won't be convenient.'

Why, she wonders, didn't they call her to warn her about it when the phone calls first started coming in?

But Mary's scared now, because she's already given out the number of the flat to that first caller.

What if he goes round there and trashes the place?

Oh my God.

She tries calling the girl who lives there, but she can't get through.

Mary considers not answering her mobile phone, but won't that make the callers even angrier? So she starts answering. She has no idea how many. Loads and loads of calls.

One asks, 'Have you ever fucked a black man?'

They're all men, except for one girl who starts off

innocently asking her where the flat is. Then out of the blue she starts comparing Mary to local landlord Nicholas Hoogstraten, who's on trial for allegedly arranging the contract killing of a business rival. 'Who?'

Mary's never heard of him. She thinks he's maybe a pop singer. She's embarrassed that she's lived here for seventeen years and has never even heard of him.

Right after that a man calls, saying in a creepy voice, 'I want room. I want room.' It gives her the shivers.

Few offer her the chance to explain that it's all a mistake. She understands why people are angry. She can't comprehend why the *Friday Ad* would think it's OK to put 'white person' anyway. She has lived abroad herself, spending years in India and Iraq; she sponsors a child called Becky in Zimbabwe.

But it's the threats of violence which really scare her. 'Don't worry,' says one person. 'I'll find you.'

The calls continue until late at night, when she finally turns off the phone. She doesn't sleep, thinking about the man who now has the flat's number. What if he went round and attacked the girl there by mistake, thinking she was the one advertising?

She decides she has to go over to the flat and check it, but it involves taking two buses. The stress makes the pain in her legs worse. She calls the *Friday Ad* and asks them to pay for a taxi; she'll keep the receipt.

They hum and haw. She gets a taxi anyway.

She tells the driver why she's having to make the journey. He says, 'Oh yeah? That's just been on the news.'

Southern FM is featuring a story about the racist advert. Mary has to call them to explain that it has been a horrible mistake. The radio station back-pedals furiously, issuing public apologies.

But the damage is done. Mary worries she'll never be able to rent her flat. She's too scared to advertise it again in case one of the people who threatened her turn up. And what if the people turning up take the advertisement seriously? What if a racist applies?

The campaigner Tony Greenstein phoned her up at the weekend. He said she should be claiming disability living allowance. She never has.

He's sending her the forms to apply for it.

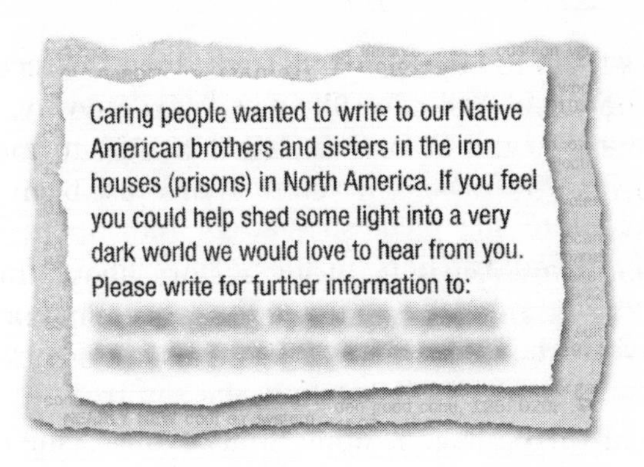

Caring people wanted to write to our Native American brothers and sisters in the iron houses (prisons) in North America. If you feel you could help shed some light into a very dark world we would love to hear from you. Please write for further information to:

When he was 13 Grandma Snowbird sent him on his vision quest.

She sent him away to a special place. She gave him a sacred pipe and some feathers, and made a circle of stones for him to sleep in, outdoors, for four nights.

There, one night, he dreamed of the sacred Iroquoi turtle. It was dancing on its hind legs, surrounded by people. The Great Spirit came and handed the turtle a feather, telling him that whoever held the feather had the right to speak.

After that Grandma Snowbird called him Turtle Dancing.

He was raised in a conventional American family in Massachusetts, but Grandma had taught him about the ways of the Iroquoi.

When his grandmother became too old and ill to look after herself she made a bargain with Turtle Dancing. If he looked after her, she would pass on as much as she knew.

So, before she died, she taught him about sweat lodges, dream catchers, medicine bags and about how everything moves in a circle. She would take him to the woods behind her house and make him sit still for an hour or two, just watching the squirrels, to teach him patience.

He tried other religions. He married and had five children. Looking back, he sees that his life then was moving in a downward spiral. His wife divorced him, alleging that he had abused their children; he has always claimed these accusations were false. 'Charges,' he says, 'that are so easily made, but so difficult to defend yourself against.'

After four months in a high-security prison they sent him to a medium-security facility. There he started attending meetings of a Native American circle. Strong men would cry, talking about their lives. The circle also campaigned for the rights of Native Americans to use the sacred pipes and smudge bowls in prison.

At first it was harrowing. One thing that kept him going was that he always had his family to write to. He was dumbfounded when he found out that many of the prisoners had no one to write to. You can't let your emotions show to other prisoners. Inside they take meekness for weakness. Everyone needs someone on the outside to talk to.

So he began arranging penpals for his fellow Native American prisoners. What shocked him was how fast the thing grew from there. It mushroomed.

It wasn't easy. Prisoners can't correspond with other prisoners, so he often had to find someone on the outside who was willing to send on letters. They weren't allowed computers either, so each letter introducing another prisoner had to be typed by hand.

A woman called Margaret from Somerset in England wrote to him. She'd been writing to death row prisoners in the USA for years, campaigning on their behalf. She'd heard from a friend about the man who'd been organizing this penpal programme for Native Americans, called Talking Leaves. Intrigued, she wrote to Turtle Dancing. When he suggested she write to another of his prisoner penpals, she said no, she wanted to correspond with him.

When she came to America to meet some of her death row penpals she came to visit him. She met his parents. He told her all about his conviction, let her read his court documents so she could judge for herself.

He was released from prison in 2000 after serving a ten-year sentence. It was frightening to be out again.

The first time he walked into a grocery store he felt the walls were closing in. A phone ringing would make him jump. He considered stopping Talking Leaves now he was a free man, but the letters kept coming.

He married Margaret. She took a Native American name – Whispering Wind. He got a job in a plastics factory, working eight hours a day. She works too. They spend their weekends keeping up with Talking Leaves.

Sometimes it's disheartening, writing to people on the inside. Four months ago a penpal in Arizona was executed. It's like losing a member of your family. But the scale of it is overwhelming. More than five hundred Talking Leaves members around the world now write to over a thousand inmates in American prisons, learning about the ways of Native Americans.

And every Sunday Turtle Dancing sits down and writes letters. Ten or fifteen of them every week.

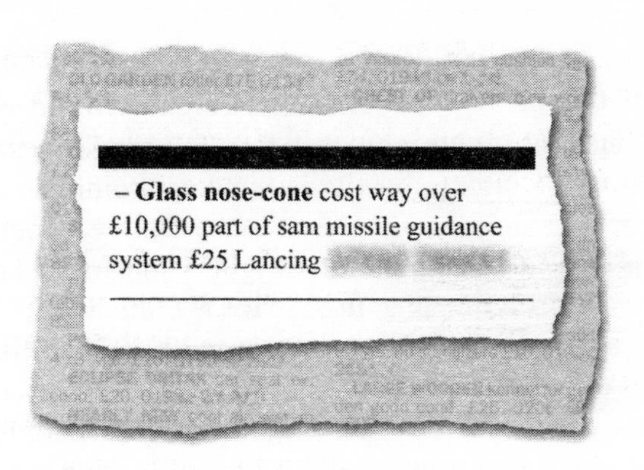

– **Glass nose-cone** cost way over £10,000 part of sam missile guidance system £25 Lancing

He was there on Christmas Island, at 17, when they tested three H-bombs and two A-bombs.

Chris had gone there with the Royal Engineers to build the runways for the tests. Afterwards, they kept the men there.

They dressed them in cotton overalls, gloves and balaclavas, and lined them up outside, about a thousand of them, while the boffins sat behind four-foot concrete walls.

The Tannoy would say, 'The bomb has left the aircraft.'

They squatted down, backs to the blast, eyes tight closed, hands over eyes. Even then you could see the light through your eyelids, and feel this incredible heat on your back. Some said they saw the bones in their hands lighting up through their skin.

'Stay down, stay down,' the Tannoy said.

You felt the blast. The wind and the sound. Palm trees lashing up and down like blades of grass. It was amazing.

In his 64 years Chris has done a lot of things.

He's one of the few men who served in all three services – the navy, the army and the air force. Twenty-six years altogether.

He'd got out of the slums of Tiger Bay as a teenager, becoming a cabin boy, sailing to South America – to ports such as Curaçao, Caracas and La Libertad. From there he joined the army, and after that the navy. For a short while he tried life as a civilian, but he missed military life.

He attempted to rejoin the army, but they wouldn't take him back. They said he was too old.

He was 24 the day he came home to tell his wife he'd joined the RAF instead. That was the day of the Aberfan disaster. Chris went up to Aberfan, trying to help dig the kids out of the slurry.

During the Falklands War he and his team of twenty-five men parachuted in to Saunders Island – 90 miles from Stanley – to set up a radar station, getting the place ready for the lads to go in. He'd been the youngest of them on Christmas Island; this time he was the oldest one in his group.

Chris was in and out. He never fired a round. It was other lads who had to do the real fighting.

In 1984 he was serving at RAF Mountbatten in Plymouth when they discovered benign tumours on his chest.

He returned to the Falklands for a tour of duty in 1985, after the war.

Given three days' R'n'R, he went back to Saunders Island. It's in Byron Sound, to the north-west of West Falkland.

He walked up the side of the hill, looking south towards Antarctica.

It felt as if he were the only person on the planet. The place was so remote that the silence was deafening. It bombarded his ears, reminding him of the roar of the wind on Christmas Island twenty-seven years earlier.

His travels have made him a hoarder. On the beach at Saunders Island he collected whalebones. He found the nose cone on the Falklands too. It was about to be thrown out. That type had been superseded, so he just happened to pick one up and put it in his naval deep-sea box, along with his whalebones, and had it shipped home.

He shouldn't have it really. It should have been destroyed. But he pocketed it, just as his grandfather had done with old shell cases, bringing them back from the war.

It is a fascinating piece of work. It's made of nine pieces of glass set on a threaded brass ring that screws on to the end of the missile. The clever thing is that they're ground and stuck together in such a way that you have perfect optical perception as you look through them, so that the instruments inside the missile can see out.

Back home his wife kept it on the window sill, using it as a terrarium.

For sixteen years he ran pubs. The first place was the Bull and Bush in Richmond.

Simon Weston – the Welsh guy who was burned in the *Sir Galahad* during the Falklands War – used to come in there sometimes.

They used to talk about it; two Welshmen who'd wound up doing different jobs in the war.

Then there was the Three Horseshoes in Lancing. They did that for eighteen months, but it was too quiet down there. Chris was bored to tears. So he packed it in and became a prison officer. 'Same customers, different bars,' he jokes.

In February he gave it up. He's 64. He and his wife were planning to retire to Cyprus; he'd served there in 1973. They were going to give up their six-bedroom house in Sussex and build a smaller three-bedroom place there instead.

Downsize. De-clutter. For months he's been selling things. He's put twenty or thirty ads in. All his old vinyl albums have gone. They fetched seven and a half thousand. The whalebones went for £10 to a guy in Chichester.

The glass nose cone had cost the RAF something like £30,000 and, after carrying it round for twenty years, he got £20 for it.

So far he's raised about £9,500 from the bits and pieces he's hoarded.

But now Cyprus is on the back burner.

He's just been diagnosed with cancer of the bladder. They've removed three tumours.

He's in the lap of the gods, he says.

It's because of Christmas Island. He's sure of it. He's been a member of the British Nuclear Tests Veterans Association for years. He goes to their annual meetings when he can, and marches with those that make it to the Cenotaph once a year. Loads of them have died. By 1999 30 per cent of the 20,000 servicemen who'd taken part in the tests in the Pacific and at Marlinga in Australia were dead; most of them were only in their fifties.

He has no doubt they were used as guinea pigs; now they're dying for it. He remembers his friend who washed down the dusty Canberras after they'd flown through the mushroom cloud to take samples. He's long, long dead.

Sometimes it makes him angry that he was just 17 when they sent him there. But he doesn't get too worked up about it. 'What's the point?'

The government and the MOD are never going to do anything to redress what happened, he believes. Besides, in those days it was blind allegiance to your queen and country. That was what made Britain great. We could do with a bit more of it these days. In the 1950s you couldn't argue. Radiation was radiation.

All those Gulf War veterans complaining. He doesn't have a lot of sympathy for them.

In October, instead of being in Cyprus, he goes back to Worthing hospital for a cystoscopy, to find out whether more tumours have grown. He's awaiting the results of the tests.

11

Never even made it to vinyl

• **Elvis Gibson Epiphone** jumbo acoustic, special ltd edition, mother of pearl, graphic pick up, with specially made hard case, stunning look and sound, cost £600, genuine reason for sale, as new, £350 or

Elvis died when Joe was 18.

By then, he'd been a fan for five years. He's never been a rich man. He came from a poor background – like Elvis.

He grew up in a depressed area of Burnley. He's done a bit of everything in his life, from driving to painting and decorating, but around the age of 40 Joe decided to become an Elvis impersonator. It was something he'd wanted to do for years. He realized that if he didn't do it soon, he'd never do it.

Elvis himself died when he was 42.

Everyone always said Joe looked like Elvis. He has the sideburns, and he dyes his hair black, just like Elvis did. He was sure he could do it. He'd seen enough Elvis impersonators over the years to believe that he could be better than most of them.

Though it was movie Elvis who first got him into it – 'Return to Sender' and all that – Joe has always inclined towards the older Elvis. Late-period Elvis. Vegas Elvis. 'Mary In The Morning' and 'It's Over' Elvis. The deep side of Elvis. He's wondered why all impersonators go for Vegas Elvis, not the younger Elvis of 'Hound Dog' and 'Blue Suede Shoes'. Maybe it's because you'd have to be a young man yourself to have that rawness.

Late-period Elvis means the suit with the sequins and the big collar. That was a problem. A lot of Elvis suits looks like clown outfits. He wanted a good one. A local dressmaker in Blackpool quoted him £350 for a basic suit. That was before you even started talking about sequins.

His wife – well, she's not really his wife, she's his partner – said: 'If you buy me a sewing machine, I'll make you one.' So he did; she made him two absolutely superb ones. A white one with tassels, and a black sequinned one. And, wanting everything to be perfect, Joe bought the guitar from Tower Music in Blackpool.

The first show he did was at a Catholic club in Lostock Hall, close by where he lives. He knew straight away that he was doing the right thing. He had a poster printed up. It says: 'Direct from little Las Vegas' – that's Blackpool – 'Memories of Elvis. Joe Delton's Songs of Elvis – Presley-style'.

He's really trying to make something of it, but there's a lot of competition. Going back a while, there weren't that many Elvis impersonators. Now there are hundreds of thousands.

Joe has dreams. He believes that when you're asleep you go off on to another plane completely. He has read a lot of books by the late medium Doris Stokes. He knows some people think that's all blah blah blah; they think all that stuff about the afterlife is all shit. But Joe believes that sleep is mixed up with death, somehow. He's a spiritual person. His brother died young; he believes he's met him in his dreams.

And he's dreamt about Elvis, too. Loads of times. In life, Elvis was surrounded by people who were awestruck. It was hard not to be. Even a superstar like Tom Jones was awestruck when he met Elvis. But it made it hard for Elvis, always being surrounded by sycophants. It makes Joe feel sad when he thinks about all the false people around Elvis. When he meets Elvis in his dreams, Joe only tries to act naturally – to be just a decent friend, rather than another hanger-on.

Joe is still struggling. That's why he's selling the guitar. He only uses it for the first two numbers. He comes on after that Zarathustra *Space Odyssey* thing and does 'CC Rider' and 'That's All Right Mama', and he strums the guitar a couple of times.

Elvis didn't really play it either. At the beginning, he wanted to do everything right. Now he realizes that's a lot of money sitting there by the side of the stage for most of the show.

He's performing at a local restaurant in a few weeks. He'd like to make the big money – go full time. But mostly, he says, it's just about giving something back to Elvis for all he's given Joe over the years. About keeping his memory alive.

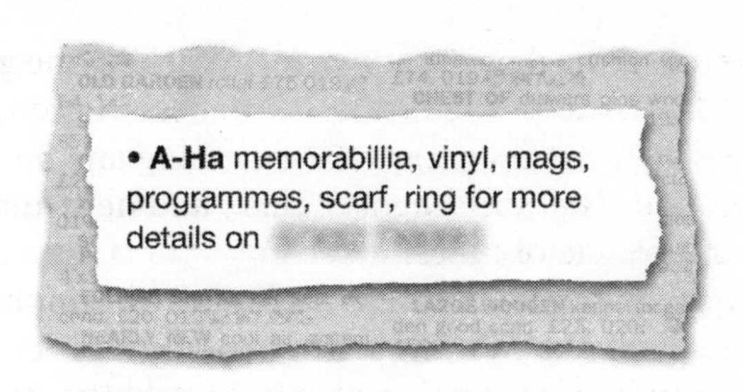
• **A-Ha** memorabillia, vinyl, mags, programmes, scarf, ring for more details on

In 1986 18-year-old David Jones started dressing like Morten Harket from A-Ha.

David had become a fan when they had their first UK hit with 'Take On Me'. When they brought that video out directed by Steve Barron – the one with the drawings of the group coming to life. It was what fans refer to as 'the third edition' of 'Take On Me'. They'd already released the song twice before.

David tied the black shoelaces around the wrist, like Morten. He bought a black leather waistcoat, pink socks, white shoes – even a black cowboy hat. Everything Morten had, David had. The gun belt. Everything.

The pharmaceutical company he worked for insisted he remove the shoelaces.

'I can't,' David said. 'I never take them off. Not even in the bath.'

It was a really good job, too, but they wouldn't let him wear them. When he refused to take them off they said, 'You've got to leave.'

A-Ha weren't just his favourite band. They were a religion.

To this day they are the only band he has ever seen play. He refused to go and see any others because it might interfere with his passion for A-Ha. Morten Harket, the good-looking singer with the falsetto voice, keyboard player Magne Furuholmen, and drummer Pål Waaktaar.

He saw them a few times. Manchester Apollo. A couple of times at Wembley.

Once, working at B&Q, he met another man who dressed as Morten. Well, David thought he looked more like John Travolta – but he was supposed to be Morten Harket. They became mates. In 1989 the two of them flew to Norway just to see the place.

They walked around Oslo with their Walkmans on, listening to the group's songs and hoping to bump into them – or people who'd known them. David bought a really expensive jumper there because it looked like one of Morten's.

Once, at Wembley, the nearest seat to the stage he could find was row 35. That wasn't good enough. He asked every single person in the front row if they'd swap their ticket with his – saying he'd throw in a few quid too. Everybody refused.

Until he came up to this other guy who was also

dressed from head to toe like Morten Harket. 'Hang on a minute, mate. My girlfriend hasn't turned up. You can sit with me.'

They ended up becoming friends too. The other guy had been dressing like Morten even before David had. They ended up going to the gigs together. Even forming a band together.

He never once met the group. He had loads of opportunities to, but he never did. Once he had a chance to see them at a small club in London; he'd have almost certainly met them there.

That was through the fan club he used to run. It started when he put a small ad in the paper looking for penpals who were into A-Ha. Soon he was getting up to a hundred letters a day, fans swapping information about Morten, Mags and Pal.

He and his penpals decided to meet up. They organized a trip to London.

All of them gathered outside Morten's house in Holland Park, peering in at a gold disc they could see on the wall. A policeman approached them, thinking they might be about to rob the place. They went to Mags's house, and Pal's. They went to places that had been shown in their videos – such as Holland Park market. And they went to Blue Sky – the café in Kensington they had named a song after, the B-side of 'Train of Thought'.

That night someone offered David a ticket to see the group at Subterranea. David turned it down, saying he couldn't because he'd have to get back to Egham that night to sleep on a friend's floor.

It was a stupid reason.

He could have caught a taxi back. It night have cost £100 but that wouldn't have mattered, because he would have met A-Ha.

For months afterwards it would keep him awake at night. 'Why didn't I go?'

Later he realized that he hadn't gone because he was afraid of meeting them there, in the small club.

'What if I did meet them – and they turned out to be a-holes?'

David wrote his own songs too. They were very influenced by A-Ha. Sometimes he'd use old song titles – ones the group had discarded.

Like David's song 'Less Than One'. That had originally been the title of 'Take On Me'.

He used to send demos of them to Norway – to the addresses he'd found for the band. He never heard anything back.

Eventually he met a girl who was a singer. She performed the songs with him. They were good. They fell in love, settled down, married and had a baby. David wanted to name the girl Daha, because it had

'A-Ha' in it, but eventually they chose something else.

On 14 February 1994 David wrote a song called 'Days On End' – the original title of A-Ha's hit 'Scandal Days'. They never used it, so David thought it was OK to take it.

It was about his wife. *'Come on baby, be mine forever, be my forever valentine... Our love for each other is a godsend/ I need you tonight, for days on end...'*

He and his wife started recording David's tunes. They pressed up CDs and sent them out. The local BBC station GMR played one track. The local music business entrepreneur Tony Wilson who ran Factory Records even called them up, enthusiastically asking for copies. There was talk of a deal with BMG.

But just when everything should have been perfect, David had a mental breakdown. He stopped work. He became jealous, wondering whether his wife had other boyfriends. Suicidal, he attempted to kill himself with an overdose. He packed up and left, losing his car, his home and his daughter. His wife refused to let him see her.

His passion hasn't waned. He listens to the song 'Rolling Thunder' full blast. It gives him goose pimples. *'If your world should crumble, yeah/ And the rain gets in/ Running through your sink/ Soaking you outside in/ The rain... see it falling/ But I don't know how long it will be/ Until the storm's over/ But I'll wait/ I will.'*

It's his favourite A-Ha song these days.

Over the last two years, as he's recovered from the breakdown, he's fought to win access to his daughter. It's cost him £10,000 in legal fees.

He'd come back from court and listen to 'Out of Blue Comes Green', tears streaming down his face.

'It just felt like I'd die soon/ Don't matter/ My eyes have seen for better/ Out of blue comes green.'

Eventually this summer, his ex-wife said he could take their daughter away for a weekend to celebrate her fifth birthday.

He's been a bit short lately, so he put the advert in to raise some cash for the trip. He owns all sorts of rarities. Unreleased demo tracks. An A-Ha fan from Liverpool arrived. 'You've got the first edition of 'Take On Me'!' the Liverpudlian said excitedly.

The man paid him £120 for some bits and pieces. David had A-Ha in South America on video. He'd found it for a couple of quid in a car boot sale. The man offered £40 for it. 'All right. As long as you tape it for me.'

It's the kind of dedication that impresses David – coming all the way from Liverpool to buy A-Ha rarities.

With the money he took his daughter to Blackpool and bought her a tracksuit. It was the first time he'd spent time with her in a year and a half. She was a little angel.

Last week he finally won the court case, guaranteeing visiting rights. He's getting back on his feet. He would like to think that one day he could reconcile with his ex.

Most of all, though, he dreams of A-Ha discovering him and recording one of his songs. He's writing a new one called 'Silver and Gold'. He's got the chords, but he needs a little more inspiration.

A-Ha are still his religion. They're still the thing that guides his life.

Second to getting his daughter back, A-Ha recording one of his songs would be better than winning any lottery.

- Old punk band, record label trying to find ex members or friends of the old London based punk band The Stereotypes, dizzydetour@ [illegible] [illegible] 9am-5pm and 6-10pm

Summer 1984 – the Midhurst Detours Scooter Club were thundering through Suffolk on the way to Skegness. Riding out in front of the thirty scooters, all looking great with their mirrors, paint jobs and fox tails flying from the aerials, was David 'Dizzy' Holmes. At 21, he was the founder of the club.

Skegness was the last rally of the season. It was raining heavily; a great summer was ending.

Dizzy had started out as a punk fan, but when he was 18 he and his mates from West Sussex had been to see this Undertones gig in London. They'd never even heard of Mods back then. The support band were called The Chords. David had watched as fans dressed in parkas arrived on their scooters. 'Christ,' he said. 'What are *this* lot?'

This was something different. Something fresh. The Chords played a brilliant gig. To this day he still loves The Chords' songs like 'In My Street' and 'The British Way of Life': '*This is the British way of life now/ I swallow my dreams with my beer/ Sunday dinner with the wife now/ 'Cause nothing new happens here...'*

Back home in Midhurst Dizzy set up his own scooter club – the Midhurst Detours. They spent that first summer travelling around to the rallies – Scarborough, Brighton, Hastings, Margate and the Isle of Wight, listening to Secret Affair, The Lambrettas and The Purple Hearts.

Dizzy was a toolmaker then, earning good money with a company that was making parts for Concorde. In 1984 he shelled out £2,000 for a race-tuned Vespa – his Amandos 225. He had the picture of Brighton beach from the back cover of The Jam's *Setting Sons* spray-painted on the side.

That was what he was riding at the head of the club that day.

He didn't see the water from the flooded field until it was too late. The scooter aquaplaned and hit the motorway barrier.

Dizzy was conscious all the time. Didn't feel any pain.

Lying there on the motorway, he knew something was wrong.

When he'd hit the reservation he'd broken his back.

He'd have been depressed about the year and a half he spent in Odstock Hospital, only there were so many others worse off than him. People paralysed from the neck down. He was only paralysed from the waist.

There were times when he was angry about what had happened. He'd been young and naive. He'd bought only the cheapest possible insurance – third party, fire and theft. He received no pay-out.

Back home in a wheelchair, he tried suing the farmer whose fields had flooded the motorway. He tried suing the police. He got nowhere.

With nothing to do, he concentrated on his hobby – collecting records. He was on benefit, but his mum lent him some money to buy a large collection, so he picked out a few for himself and advertised the rest in *Scootering* magazine.

Pretty soon he was in the mail-order business, selling punk and Mod obscurities. By that time Mod was a dirty word in Britain, but the Japanese loved it. Japanese tourists used to come to visit him.

In 1992 a Margate band called The Persuaders sent him a demo tape. Three-piece; very Jam-influenced. Dizzy loved it, but the labels all shunned them, so he set up his own Detour label to put it out.

Ten years later, still in Midhurst, he's released seventy-five singles and around fifty albums. He's even put out one by The Chords.

He set up a punk label too, Binliner, releasing records no one noticed first time around. Dizzy will find some EP of which a band pressed up only fifty copies at the time. Some tracks are so obscure they never even made it to vinyl first time around. He puts on gigs for these bands sometimes too: middle-aged men having a great time, trying to remember tracks they last played twenty years ago.

Dizzy lives for late 1970s and early 1980s music. He's married to an old scooter club member, Tania, who helps him run the label.

Sometimes she tells him: 'You've got to get out of the past.' But he's obsessed.

He's working on *Bored Teenagers 3* right now – a compilation. He spends ages tracking down former members to ask permission to re-release tracks. When he finally finds them they're gobsmacked: 'Who put you up to this?' they ask, suspiciously.

Once, a guy from a band called Discharge from Sheffield assumed it was a wind-up, shouted, 'Eff off!' and put the phone down.

He hasn't found The Stereotypes yet. He's discovered one band with that name from Oxford, but they say it's not them.

• **Abba tribute bands**, experienced female vocalist looking for full time work, can do both parts of Frida and Agnetha, not available for dep work, no timewasters, Samantha

It was *Stars in Their Eyes* that took her dream away.

It was 1996 and Samantha had auditioned to be Barbra Streisand singing 'Somewhere'.

On the Wednesday Granada called up and told her she'd got through and would be appearing on the show. She'd cracked it.

If *Stars in Their Eyes* wasn't enough, that same week she'd also passed the audition for Michael Barrymore's *My Kind of People*, but when she told them she was on *Stars in Their Eyes* as well, the Barrymore people said she couldn't be on both – she'd have to choose. She told them thanks, but she'd rather do *Stars in Their Eyes*.

Then on the Friday, Granada phoned again. We're really sorry, but we don't need as many performers as we'd originally thought. They were hoping to squeeze twelve more singers into the schedule but were told they couldn't.

They said to Samantha they'd put twelve names into a hat and pulled out nine. Hers wasn't one of the names they'd chosen.

'But you told me I was going to be on the show.'

She rang *My Kind of People.*

The producer said, 'You're too late. Booked somebody else.'

That night, Samantha hit the bottle. She opened the brandy and put on her Supertramp record, listening to the singer telling her that she was just a dreamer, a stupid little dreamer.

She'd left school at 16 with no exams. Good-looking girl. Could sing well. That was when she started doing it professionally in cover bands.

The best time had been with a group called the Professionals. Their act was based around doing impressions of other bands. Samantha was the main person. She'd be doing Blondie one minute, then come off, and while one of the boys filled in with a bit of Billy Idol she'd be changing into a Bee Gees costume.

She was in her twenties and it was brilliant. They'd tour army bases in Germany and she'd be up drinking every night, surviving on four hours' sleep.

It was after the Professionals split up that she went for *Stars in Their Eyes.* All the time she'd known she was going to be famous.

After the mix-up she realized that it was never going to happen to her. She'd ballsed it up. She'd failed.

What made it harder was that her sister got on *Stars in Their Eyes* not long after she was dropped. She was Tina Arena. The annoying thing was that Samantha's sister had never been as ambitious as she was. Samantha used to go on and on at her to try harder at singing. Her sister had been married, and had kids. Samantha never did that. She was saving herself for her career. And then her sister auditioned and got on.

People were coming up to Samantha, confused. 'Is that you going to be on *Stars in Their Eyes*?'

'No,' she'd say through gritted teeth. 'It's my sister.'

She could have gone and sat in the audience to watch her, but she couldn't face doing it.

It was just bad luck.

After that she worked up her own act, the Samantha Allen Experience. She's a one-woman cabaret act performing humorous impressions of other singers. She can do thirty-two different impressions.

Anyone new comes out and she'll shut herself away with the videotape and play it over and over again to get the voice and the look and all the mannerisms. Then she changes the lyrics around a bit. Alison Moyet sings about her weight. Kylie Minogue sings about her bum.

On stage, she'll turn around and put a false arse on and then she's Kylie – or she puts a satellite dish on her head and pretends to be Sophie Ellis Bextor. It's a bit like Bobby Davro, only with singing. Geri, Celine Dion, Blondie, Boy George, the Gibb brothers... she does them all. She bases it on a Freddie Starr routine, and she'll be happy if she's half as funny as he is.

But she's 35 now. She doesn't want to be famous any more anyway. She'd rather be Samantha Allen than Geri Halliwell.

She imagines what it would be like to be 50 and still singing in working men's clubs. Singing doesn't do what it used to for her any more. She regrets sacrificing herself.

She has never had a long-term stable relationship with a man. They get fed up with her working every weekend. She wanted children, and she realized she was running out of time.

Last year she found herself depressed, sitting in a working men's club in Warrington.

Being on your own is tougher than being in a band. You set up the gear yourself. There's no one to talk to, because the audience are always in couples and a lot of the women get jealous if you talk to their husbands. You get a rough audience and they will let you know, and there's no one there to gee you up.

The Warrington audience had been horrible and unappreciative. She'd had enough. An agent had come to see her and it all poured out. She said: 'I'm fed up. I haven't got a man in my life and I have no children. I need a normal life.'

She hates it so much. The people. The job. She's had enough.

She remembers somebody telling her about Maxine Barry. She's a singer who made it. You know, the one who does Shirley Bassey? She won *Stars in Their Eyes* in 1992. When she sung she'd always get the audience up on their feet, shouting and clapping. But she said she'd always drive home on her own. In tears. Because she had no life.

After Warrington, Samantha decided to get out of showbiz. She signed up for an HND in computing. It has been really hard. She doesn't even have O-levels. Other people studying have spent their lives working in offices; she was on stage. But she's passed, and she's proud of it.

Now she's looking for part-time work doing second-line support for companies. That's where the cash is. She lives in Chester and she knows people who are on thirty-five grand a year, which is really good money up north.

And she's in a relationship now. 'He's in IT, funnily enough,' she says.

But he used to play in bands when he was younger too, so he understands what she's been through.

Much as she'd like to, she can't afford to give up music straight away. In the meantime, maybe she can find work in an ABBA tribute band. Just mid-week gigs, maybe. The audience would all be ABBA fans, so they'd be up for it. Not like the working men's clubs where the audiences are sat there with their arms crossed: 'Show us what you can do.'

Today she sat an exam for an IT course she's been doing. She passed. Level 3 Computing.

She's happy now. She's in love. Once, she had thought she was going to be a famous singer. It just didn't work out.

12

Let's get a dog

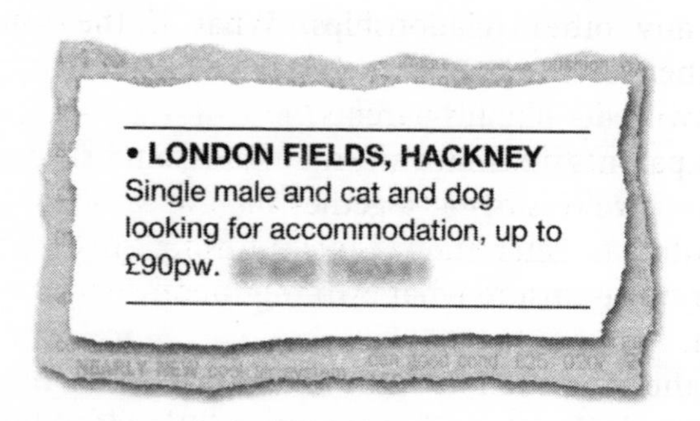

• **LONDON FIELDS, HACKNEY**
Single male and cat and dog looking for accommodation, up to £90pw.

At 16 Peter met Nicky in Northampton. He was still at school. They fell in love but their parents didn't approve so they ran off together.

They were still together in their mid-twenties, and everything was running smoothly. He'd got a job, a home, a partner. One day they said: 'Let's get a dog.'

The advert in the pet shop said: 'Puppies. Border collie crosses. Free to a good home.'

They weren't collies at all, they were Belgian Shepherds – like Alsatians, only black, and a good few inches taller. Big dogs. They chose one and their friends said they should call him Zebedee because of the way he bounced up and down.

Everything seemed almost perfect. The way things were going, it probably wouldn't be long before he and Nicky had children.

That thought scared him. Neither of them had ever had any other relationships. What if they stayed together for the rest of their lives and became bitter and twisted – like his parents?

His parents' marriage wasn't a good one. They used to say: 'We're staying together for the kids.' And so, according to Peter, the kids went through hell instead. He grew up unsure what love was, because he'd never felt it.

In the year after they acquired Zeb, Peter became depressed. He felt as if there was a little black hole in his heart, with all the love spilling out of it. He could love people, but couldn't accept other people's love.

One day he said to Nicky: 'Shall we see what the world is like on our own?' They cried a lot and held each other, but she agreed.

She had scoliosis – curvature of the spine – and couldn't handle a big dog like Zeb by herself. One tug from him and she'd be on her back for a week. So Peter kept the dog and one of their three cats – the one they called Dylan.

But Nicky and Peter stayed close. Peter worked delivering cars; if he was late home, Nicky would look after Zeb.

After a couple of years, she fell in love with another man. Next thing she was having a baby. Peter didn't want to stay around to see how things turned out. So at 30 he gave the cat to his dad to look after and he went travelling with Zebedee. At first he travelled around Britain, and then started working his way around Europe. In Andorra he helped out at a ski resort for a while. He cleared gardens, or did a bit of housework.

People were good to him and Zebedee. In return for work farmers would let them spend the night in their barns, or pitch a tent in their fields. Peter returned home happy, with a wonderful view of humanity.

But now he's 33 and he feels he needs to move on, instead of always worrying where the next meal is coming from. And Zeb is eight. Peter notices the dog's back foot slipping sometimes; Belgian Shepherds can be prone to hip problems. He used to be able to walk 7, 8 miles without worrying. Now half an hour walking round Victoria Park and he's exhausted.

'So right,' Peter says to himself. 'Find somewhere and settle.'

But with a dog it's hard to find anywhere. His mother was the first of many to tell him he should rehouse the dog, but he's stubborn. Zeb wouldn't like it. You wouldn't rehouse a child just because they were inconvenient, would you?

Peter has already spent a year living on the floor of his 84-year-old father's flat. This February he moved to London, staying at a friend's. Zeb would sit by the door, whining when Peter went out to work. He'd pull his own fur out.

'He's depressed,' his friend said. 'He misses you.'

After a couple of weeks she told him, 'I know I said you could stay, but I can't cope with the dog.'

'All right. I'll find somewhere else.'

He looks through all the papers. He's spoken to 140 people. Some sound enthusiastic until they see the size of the dog, and the thickness of his fur. 'Oh. He's a bit large.'

They say: 'Sorry. Seemed like a good idea, but it's too much hassle, mate...'

If anyone tries to tell him that his loyalty to Zeb is all mixed up with the way his relationship broke up he can only agree. Definitely. Zeb is the only link to the past he's got. He understands that.

He hasn't spoken to Nicky in years but he thinks about her every single day. Sometimes he hears about her from friends.

He's done things in his life he's regretted; he knows he'd regret rehousing Zeb for the rest of his life so he's not going to, and that's that. What was it George Bernard Shaw said? The more things a man is ashamed of, the more respectable he is. OK. Given the choice between respectability and shame, knows which he'd choose.

Last night, the friend of a friend whose house he's staying in said: 'You can stay as long as you want.' Peter knows he's only saying that.

So he's moving back into a tent. Dropping out again. 'It'll only be until Zebedee's days are done. Then,' he promises, 'I'll drop back in.'

LOST DOG LARGE REWARD
Leading to the whereabouts of our
3 year old male Weimaraner lost near
Priest & University on 10/17/03
PLEASE HELP US
FIND OUR PET

Craig had had a Weimaraner when he was a kid. It had been born a couple of days before Craig, and it had died on his 14th birthday.

He'd loved that dog.

And he loved Shultz, the Weimaraner he'd bought three years ago from a small farm in Wellsville, Kansas.

In October last year 31-year-old Craig and Shultz left Kansas City to visit a friend in Tempe, Arizona, for a few days.

Three days after arriving, Craig decided to spend a weekend in Chicago so – rather than take the dog on an air trip – he left Schultz at the friend's house.

On the Sunday morning Craig was about to catch the flight back from O'Hare airport when the call came through on his cell phone.

On Saturday night someone had left the gate of the friend's yard open. Shultz and the friend's own dog had disappeared.

There was a security crackdown at O'Hare. The queues were so long Craig missed his flight. He didn't make it home until night-time.

It was heart-wrenching knowing all the time Shultz was gone and he couldn't do anything about it. He felt horrible.

The friend who had been looking after the dog was upset.

Craig was really mad at him. He felt he should have been out there looking for Schultz instead of staying there, crying.

Craig closed up his house in Kansas City and moved to Arizona to search for his dog. Shultz meant everything to him. He wasn't leaving Arizona without him.

Every day for three months Craig trawled the streets, searching, handing out flyers. He stretch-necked at cars, checking out the dogs. He called the pounds twice a day. He talked to the Boys and Girls Club and offered them a big reward. It was hell.

One day somebody called and said there was a stray Weimaraner wandering around in an alleyway. Craig dashed up there.

It wasn't Shultz. Craig caught the dog and turned him into the pound. When nobody claimed him, Craig drew lots for him and won him. Moose was a really loving dog, about a year old, but he wasn't a substitute for Shultz.

He put classified advertisements in the local papers.

He travelled up to Sedona to consult a psychic. Crazy stuff. Nothing worked.

Each week the ads got bigger and bigger. Finally he wrote a really sappy ad. 'Reward $1500. Missing Weimaraner. 3 yr old male. Please return my child. I am lost without him.'

The paper picked up the story and put it on the front page. 'Love Unleashed. Owner moves to state to find dog.'

Dave works in a shop on the other side of the junction from the house where Shultz was staying when he ran away. Dave found the dog wandering around outside the store, confused.

He took Shultz back to his home in Mesa. For three months Shultz lived there with Dave, his fiancée and their two toddler children. They loved Shultz too.

But friends of Dave's started calling up about this piece they'd read in the *Republic*. They knew it was Dave's new dog. There was a $1,500 reward. 'Dude, that's a lot of money. Just turn him in.'

Dave was broke. He had only $11 in his checking account. All the same, he refused even to think about it; he just couldn't do it.

But the story of Craig's missing Weimaraner kept growing. The following Sunday was country DJ Kris Lamb's last radio show on KMLE-FM 107.9 before he moved away to Nashville. He wanted a big gimmick to go out on, so he called Craig up for an interview, stoking up the story. 'Come on! Let's all get together. We can help this guy out.'

A woman from Scottsdale called up and offered another $500 to add to the reward.

Then a listener called. He said he was sure he'd seen Shultz. By the end of the show they'd tracked Dave down. On air, Dave and Craig spoke for the first time.

Finally, reluctantly, Dave agreed to give up the dog.

The next day, Craig was at Dave's door in Mesa. Shultz recognized him instantly, jumping up at the big window beside the front door.

Craig spent $8,500 looking for the dog – including the $1,500 reward he was giving to Dave – but it was worth it.

Dave was standing there, crying.

Craig was crying too. Both of them, crying and crying. And Shultz going nuts, so excited he was sneezing.

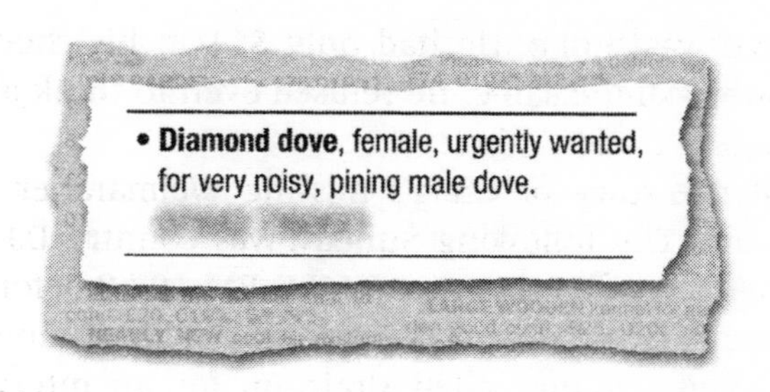

• **Diamond dove**, female, urgently wanted, for very noisy, pining male dove.

Alan has known Mark since he was about 5. Mark's ten years older. Back then Alan would take Mark down to the local stream.

'If you see a shark,' Mark would say, handing him a stick, 'hit it.'

And, like a fool, Alan would stand there, waiting.

One day, when Alan was about 6, he found Mark standing in his garden with the rung of a ladder.

'Help me out here,' said Mark. 'I could do with growing a ladder, only I haven't got the time.'

'You can't grow ladders,' said Alan.

''Course you can.'

'Get away.'

Mark had Alan watering a rung he'd placed in the earth. The next day, Alan goes round to Mark's house and there's this great big ladder sticking out of the ground.

Alan walks round to the front door: 'It's worked!'

Their friendship has been like that for thirty-five years – Mark playing these tricks on Alan. It never stops.

They grew up. Mark worked on the oil rigs. Alan became a financial consultant. Towards the end of last year Alan realized that their friendship was drifting. He mentioned this to the woman he lives with. 'Why don't you get some common interest,' she suggested. 'What does Mark like doing now?'

'He's got this aviary,' said Alan. 'I'm certainly not getting into that!' Never had any interest in birds whatsoever, Alan. 'Can't be bothered with them, to be honest,' he'd say. Birds were for the sky.

But she said: 'Go round and see him anyway.'

So he did, and Mark took him down to his aviary. Some chicks had just hatched, and he was preparing some other birds for auction. Alan watched, fascinated. His friend seemed to get so much pleasure from it.

'Tell you what,' said Mark. 'Try a couple of Japanese quails. See what you think.'

They're small ground birds – lovely to look at. Mark gave them to Alan and said, 'You feed 'em a bit of corn and that's it.'

'OK,' said Alan. 'Fair enough.'

That's how it started, seven months ago. From there he got some Kakarikis – lovely green miniature parrots from New Zealand originally. He got them from the papers. *Kakarikis for sale. Young. £20.* After that, it was Java sparrows.

Little did he know that the reason Mark was getting rid of the Japanese quails was that they're not very happy about being with other birds. They attack them. That was why Mark was so keen to get rid of them.

So Alan had to get rid of them too.

Mark and Alan were sitting in Alan's back garden the other day when Mark heard these birds chattering.

'What did you say you'd done with them Japanese ones?' Mark asked.

Alan burst out laughing.

'I don't believe it. You just put them in your neighbour's back garden, didn't you?'

Together, he and Mark started going to bird auctions.

'Unbelievable,' said Alan, seeing people bid five hundred quid for an African Grey. Mynahs go for three hundred. And the varieties and the colours are just fantastic.

It opened up a new world for him. Now he goes to the bottom of the garden to his aviary a few times a day to take a look. Before he got into birds he would have thought it iffy behaving like his, but there is one particular Java sparrow he's got that comes straight up to the wire whenever he approaches and bursts into song. And it's beautiful. He knows it sounds daft, but...

Mark was round one day when his Java sparrow was singing. He was impressed too. 'Oh, I've got to get some of those,' he said.

A Kakariki's song isn't quite so attractive. They make a noise like a bleating sheep.

Alan bumped into his neighbour in the street recently. The man said: 'I'm not being funny, but I keep hearing this goat.'

Alan feigned surprise: 'I've heard that too. I was wondering if you were keeping one.'

Mark came round the other day with this Diamond dove, a tiny little thing, the size of a sparrow.

'The female has flown off and he's driving the neighbours mad calling for her,' he told Alan. 'I've only got a small place. D'you mind keeping her for a bit?'

'Yeah, no problem,' said Alan.

At 4.30 the next morning he understood why Mark had been so keen to get rid of it. *Coo. Coo. Coo.* Nightmare. It was unbelievable.

Mark had pulled another one on him. Typical. Just like he used to when they were kids.

At five, Alan called Mark.

'Hello?'

'I called so you could listen to your dove.' *Coo. Coo. Coo.*

Mark just laughed.

It'd shut up if they found a female for it. That's all it's shouting for. They've tried looking, but they only sell them in tens at auctions.

Another neighbour collared Alan and said: 'Have you heard that wood pigeon?'

'I have.' Alan tutted. 'Blimey. Isn't it terrible?'

Alan says to Mark: 'You'd better bloody sort this out and get a female, otherwise we'll have to work out whether it's a homing pigeon or not.'

And there's Mark, laughing still.

It was hooting away again at 4.15 this morning.

Alan's got a plan. There's a bird auction in Knutsford on the first Wednesday of every month. He's going to go there to look for a mate. If he doesn't find one, he's going to buy ten males.

And sneak round to Mark's aviary and put them all in there.

See how funny he finds that.

• VERMIN CONTROL. DEER RABBIT & FOXES culled and controlled to your requirements quickly and discreetly. Carcases removed if required, lamping possible for foxes and rabbits. 30 years of experience in total, no fee for our time or ammunition, although a voluntary contribution for fuel if over 40 miles is not unwelcome. Please call Robin on Evenings or Days

He's sitting in a hedge doing nothing except watching the clouds go by. It's cold and windy, but it's an escape to be here in the middle of nowhere.

He'll get home after work in the evening from his job in Oxford and wonder, Can I escape to do a bit of shooting?

Or he'll go out in the early morning before the ramblers arrive – because there are people who don't like coming across a man with a rifle on his arm. They'll tut-tut. He'll bet they'll eat a nice bit of venison when they get to a restaurant, though, but that's another matter.

Besides, there are criminals everywhere these days so you can't go waving guns around. So he'll look around carefully before he pulls his .243 Winchester out of the car.

Got a couple of shotguns, but he doesn't like the bloody things. A big bang, a load of recoil and no guarantee you've killed cleanly.

He's one of the few riflemen whose gun licence allows him to shoot on land anywhere in the UK, if the farmer invites him. Mostly it's deer. With reds – which you find more in Scotland – and fallow and roe, there are seasons when he's permitted to hunt. The only deer that has no season is the muntjac – it escaped from Woburn Park in the 1920s, and though they're only the size of a medium-sized dog they're turning up everywhere, even in town gardens. He'll shoot foxes and rabbits at night if a farmer wants – 'lamping' them, shining a bright light into their eyes to dazzle them.

But it's deer which are the biggest pest. Years ago you'd never see them. Now he spots three or four every morning on the drive to work. Not always alive, either. Sometimes they're splattered on the road, surrounded by broken glass.

One desperate farmer he's working for has thirty thousand new trees being systematically destroyed by roes. He pays Robin £20 for each one he kills.

When Robin shoots one he cuts off its head, puts it in a cold-storage box near the farmer's house. The farmer counts the heads and then pays him.

Robin doesn't let the carcasses go to waste. He eats them, gives them to friends, or sells them to a game dealer. It's not like the stuff you buy in the supermarkets, pumped full of rubbish.

It's about the hunt.

They say a deer can count your eyelashes at 100 yards. Their senses of smell and hearing are pretty sharp too.

He'll spot a deer 600 yards away, but you need to be within 200 to ensure a clean kill. Plus a bullet will travel 5 kilometres and it's lethal up to about 4 – so you need to know where the bullet will go if you miss. Not that he misses much. About once a year.

The point is that when you don't see its legs waving in the air and you know it's dropped dead on the spot you can say to yourself, 'Yeah. I've done the job.'

Often they'll bolt before you get anywhere near.

So it's a surprise today, sitting in the hedge, when he spots it.

A roe deer, walking straight in line with him.

It hasn't even seen him.

He raises the rifle quietly.

It's only 100 feet away. Incredible.

He holds his breath.

13
Topsoil

– The owners of Green Island in Choiseul Sound wish to thank 78 Squadron and JOC at Mount Pleasant, and in particular the Sea King and Chinook helicopter flight crews and coordinators for their concerted effort in dealing with the recent fire on the island. Sally and Jerome Poncet, Beaver Island.

They first arrived in the Falklands on their 51-foot schooner *Damien II* in 1979. As a yachtsman, Frenchman Jerome was already famous for his five-year voyage around the world in the original *Damien*. Raised in Tasmania, Sally was a biologist. *Damien II* was Sally and Jerome Poncet's home. They raised three boys aboard her.

Impressed by the people and the remoteness of the islands, they returned in 1983, using them as a base while working on wildlife surveys in the Antarctic and South Georgia. They are experts in these waters.

In the post-war 1980s the government was splitting up the big company-owned farms. They were selling off uninhabited islands for as little as £1,000. As conservationists, Jerome and Sally bought around two dozen small islands, including Beaver Island, an isolated sheep farm off the south-west coast of West Falkland which became their family home. Where possible they removed sheep and allowed the local tussac grass to return.

This summer, Sally is winding up three months on South Georgia, 800 miles to the east, completing the first albatross census of the entire island. All three local species are in rapid decline, killed by the hooks of long-line trawlers. Her team are camping out on the island. Every day they check in on HF radio with the administrative centre at King Edward Point. One January morning they have a message; there is a fire on Green Island.

It's one of theirs. About 1.5 kilometres long at the entrance to Mare Harbour in East Cove, Green Island is pristine. It has never been farmed. It's one of the few remaining rat-free islands, and as such home to birds like Cobb's wren, a local species that only survives in areas without rats and cats.

Eight hundred miles away, Sally knows immediately it will be bad. The tussac grass, which grows in mounds up to 2 metres high, at this time of year is like a large dry bale of hay.

The first to spot the fire were the military at Mount Pleasant, a base established after the Falklands War. For six hours until the light went, they flew Sea Kings and Chinooks over the fire, dumping water from giant buckets on to the flames. It's frustrating being so far away, but Sally knows they did as much as she could expect.

But tussac grass sits on peat that can burn underground, unnoticed, for months – even for years sometimes. And the fires do break out again in the following days. Wind sweeps them across the island. Sally gets reports. 'There was still some green last week. But it's all gone now, apparently.' The entire island has burned.

Suspicion falls on a group of tourists who visited the island the day before the fire was spotted. Tourism here has exploded in the last few years. In 1995 there were five thousand cruise ship tourists; this year they're expecting fifty thousand. But there is little to be gained in pointing the finger.

At the weekend, Sally will visit Green Island for the first time since coming home. She will discover how bad things are. Tussacbirds, pipits and meadowlarks will have escaped, but burrowing petrels will have been killed, and that's a significant loss. She's hoping the sea lions will have all made it to the water.

If the fire is out, the island will slowly regenerate over decades. The danger is that the fires underground will reduce the soil to ash. If that blows away it leaves bare rock. The environment is lost for ever.

She is not looking forward to it. All that will be left is the charred tussac. Peat fires leave deep burning holes. It can be almost volcanic.

Occasionally you wonder whether it's a completely futile business. It might be simpler doing an ordinary job. The upside of life here is still to be able to know places such as South Georgia.

She'd give anything to be spending another three months there.

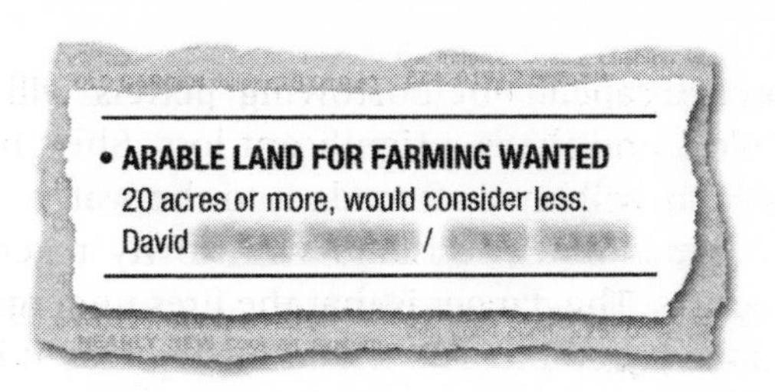
• **ARABLE LAND FOR FARMING WANTED**
20 acres or more, would consider less.
David /

In the Nyanga mountains, David's father harvests peaches from a thousand trees. He grows cabbages for seed, too. Though other farmers in Nyanga have copied him, his father was the first to grow these crops on top of a cool mountain in the east of Zimbabwe.

Growing up there, David inherited his father's love for agriculture. Fifteen years ago, he himself was raising his own crops of potatoes on 100 acres of land.

But he was a journalist, too, working for a magazine called *Read On*. Set up by radicals to promote adult literacy, it had a social agenda supporting unions and activists. Once, David interviewed Morgan Tsvangerai for it, not long after he'd become secretary-general of the Zimbabwe Congress of Trade Unions. Now he's the leader of Zimbabwe's opposition.

When he and some colleagues realized they were being followed by Mugabe's security agents, David just found it exciting. Once they chased him and his friends through the streets until they made it to the safety of a police station. His colleagues took the event more seriously than David did. But he was young; it was a thrill.

Besides, the security men were just trying to scare them. Maybe they'd lock you up, but that was all. That happened to David's own brother – also a journalist. This was before journalists started being tortured, and even killed.

In 1991, David came to Britain; a brother who was living here encouraged him to stay. Even then it wasn't about security, though David wonders what would have become of him if he had remained in Zimbabwe.

He tried to continue as a journalist here. He enrolled at the London School of Journalism and did some freelance work, but though granted indefinite leave to stay he has never found a full-time job. Being black plays a large part in that, he believes.

Britain has disappointed him. He is still trying; he doesn't want to lose hope.

He has decided to try farming instead of journalism. Last year, with a wife and three kids now, he moved from north London out to Essex, to be able to afford a house with a decent garden. In it, he planted white maize, like they grow in Zimbabwe. Similar to sweetcorn, but the taste is different. David misses the taste; it's a personal thing. Just as the water in other countries never tastes as good as it does at home.

His wife encourages him. 'Why not go for it?' she says.

He's sure there's a market. The trouble is finding the land. He needs 100 acres, but he's struggling to find even one or two. Again he thinks it's because he is black. They hear his accent or his name, Mwanka, and can't believe he knows how to farm here.

'I want to grow maize,' he told one landowner.

'Maize! You must be dreaming. Not in this country.'

Yet white maize grows easily here. He's researched it and until thirty years ago it used to be a British crop. He shows the doubters the cobs he's grown in his back garden; they say he must have bought them at a market.

One man offered 126 acres in Milton Keynes, but the land hadn't been farmed for years. Locals were used to walking on it. What would they think if he fenced it off? And him being a black person, too?

Being Zimbabwean, David sees the irony. There, land is a big issue – though it's not really about land at all. Mugabe talks of redistribution because his politics have failed; it's the last card he has to play.

They're putting people on the land there who have no idea how to farm. And even without redistribution, David could have all the land he needs in the Nyanga mountains.

It's here that he feels excluded.

14
This is what I want to do

• **RELINQUISH CONTROL!!**
To the illustrious Mistress Eloise, discreet.
Strictly by appointment. Brighton

It started after a row.

Her boyfriend wouldn't admit he *was* her boyfriend. That was the problem. It was really winding her up.

And being young and vindictive, Eloise thought she'd go and befriend an old girlfriend of his – one he always told her he hated. Eloise knew that would really upset him.

Besides, she was curious. This ex of his worked as a domme – a dominatrix – running her own fetish shop in Kemptown.

Eloise had left home only a few weeks earlier to study maths at the University of Sussex. She was just 18 – sexually pretty innocent. She'd grown up in a very small town. Home counties. *Very* conservative. Sort of place where if you're not 35 you're not allowed an opinion.

But the idea of bondage had always made her go weak at the knees.

She can't tell you why BDSM excited her. It's beyond analysis, she insists.

Terrified, she walked into the ex's fetish shop and this bolshie larger-than-life Scottish domme called Mistress Amber bounded out from nowhere. Eloise let her curiosity show, so Mistress Amber offered to show Eloise the ropes.

Eloise remembers her nerves the first time she took part in one of Mistress Amber's dungeon sessions. She was shaking – visibly. For all she's witnessed subsequently, she's never been as shocked as she was then, seeing that man chained to a cage door. Gagged. Clamps on his nipples. The lot.

She felt sick.

Yet walking home afterwards, she felt a surge of absolute elation – the sensation of finding something that you realize you've been looking for a long time. And she'd been *paid* for it.

For a week, she ran around telling her friends: 'You won't *believe* what I've just done…'

Seven years later she's still doing it. She worked with Amber all through university. Some clients are shy so she says: 'You're not going to shock me, because there is *nothing* I haven't seen before.'

After university she worked as a computer programmer; she didn't really enjoy it. It was driving her insane. She was doing an occasional dungeon session with Amber, or a bit of maid training, just to keep her hand in.

Then, last summer, she was halfway through doing something despicable to a man in Croydon – it was really disgusting – and right there she had an epiphany.

She realized, 'Yeah! *This* is what I want to do!'

It's not about being a dom, or a sub. To her those things are interchangeable. What it's really about is deviancy. That's what she likes about it.

And having serious control over these people. It's not really about making money at all. It's about standing there and looking beautiful, saying, 'Worship me.' And people do. Which always surprises her. It's a great ego trip.

OK, so sometimes it's like any job. There's a client you don't like. Or someone who's malodorous.

But as a dominatrix you're always within your rights to say, 'How dare you come and see me smelling like that? Go home and have a shower and then come back and see me.'

And then when they come back you get to hit them. It's one of the things that distinguishes a good mistress from a bad one. You've got to be someone who can hit without thinking, 'Ow. That's going to hurt.'

Of course, sometimes she gets sick of it, and almost finds herself longing for a bit of normality.

Her mobile phone rings. She has two – one for professional purposes.

She advertises in *Forum* and *Exchange & Mart*. *E&M* is where all the pervs go. She's tried the *Friday Ad* a few times but you mostly get sniffers from there. They phone for a bit of a chat then never turn up.

She checks the number to see whether she recognizes it.

It's her slave checking in. He's nearly 40, he's not attractive, yet they have an oddly intimate relationship. He has signed a three-month contract that requires him not to do pretty much anything without her say-so. She smiles. It's hard work for him because she's never happy.

She got an email yesterday from a domme who's had this slave for years. She can't keep him any more. Can Eloise take him off her hands? Slaves can get passed from mistress to mistress and master to master. It's a completely different world. Part of the fun is that it's hush-hush.

A slave contract. That's the ultimate.

Eloise isn't her real name. It's from the song by the Damned. It upsets her, sometimes, when she realizes she's lying to her mother about what she does. Not that she'd mind – it's her father she wants to keep the truth from.

Relationships with boys are no easier these days. She'd like someone who could give her a cuddle and to watch *EastEnders* with. But being a domme destroys relationships. It creates a wall.

She's seeing someone right now, and as far as the deviance thing goes he's fine. Whenever she gets a new toy he's first in line to try it out. It's just the whole thing about doing this for a living.

Guys don't like the fact that she does this stuff with other men, and for money.

Now she's building herself a new dungeon under a jewellery shop. The walls are festooned with whips and strange devices. Her clients usually buy the toys. One arrived with a speculum recently. Sometimes she wonders: Am I really doing this? Is this *real*?

The other day she went to a timber yard and bought a large, thick, seasoned timber beam. 'What d'you want it for, love?' the man at the lumber yard asked her innocently.

Eloise has sawn it in half and bolted the two pieces together to form a St Andrew's cross – a large X shape – to strap clients to. She steps back happily. 'Quite proud of that,' she says.

LAPDANCE across the world. Just name the country and you could dance there, over 20 destinations worldwide! Experienced dancers and beginners welcome. Great travel, great money. To apply send TWO recent photos stating experience to: X-Factor Model Management, PO Box 675, [illegible] or email xfactorladies@[illegible] or ring Ena on [illegible]

After the journalism course there just wasn't anything out there.

Ena ended up working for her local paper in Somerset. It wasn't exactly her. Interviewing farmers and writing about how to stop weeds growing in your garden bored her half to death.

There was an advert in *The Stage*; a TV presenting job. She'd qualified in TV journalism so she sent off her CV. Only when they contacted her to offer an interview did she realize that it was for an adult channel.

'Oh my God.'

But she went along all the same. She did the interview and the screen test.

'God. What have I done?'

There was a female porn star at the interview who, it turned out, was also an agent representing adult actresses. Ena was curious. She started talking to her and the channel's owner, asking them questions about the business and how it worked, and found she got along well with them.

That's where the idea came from.

She's a well-brought-up, well-spoken middle-class girl, but she has always been fascinated by women who make their living in the adult industry. She's not someone who's owned loads of porn herself, but she's open minded. She doesn't think there's anything wrong with it.

As she listened to what they were saying she began to realize that this was an industry she could earn a lot of money in. She was looking for something that was going to make her rich, and journalism wasn't it.

The adult channel offered her the job, but by then Ena had already decided she didn't want it. She didn't really like the idea of her parents flicking past Sky One with the remote and suddenly coming across their daughter hosting porn films on an adult channel. But it was possible to be in the industry without being on screen. She could have a back-seat role.

Very single-mindedly, she started building up her own contacts in the industry. Here her journalism training finally came in handy. To kick things off, she did some solo action photos herself for some of Paul Raymond's magazines. This was OK. Her parents don't look at top-shelf magazines.

She'd counted without the magazine using her real name, though, and without someone local spotting the photos. Next thing everyone in the little Somerset village where she lives knew what she was up to. Until then Ena had been this angelic girl who lived next to the vicar. Right opposite the village church.

She's not embarrassed. Some people actually respect her for what she does. Her friend Mali – a beauty therapist – had always been intrigued by the sex industry. When Ena needed to find a model to send to LA for a photo shoot she approached her. 'That sounds really interesting,' Mali said. She wanted to do more than just be a model. 'Why don't you come round tomorrow,' Mali said, 'and I'll work out how much I can put into the business.'

They formed a partnership. Surfing the Internet, Ena discovered an agency in Japan that was looking for lap dancers. Soon they were supplying dancers for clubs in Spain, Portugal, Iceland and America. They've just sent some to a club in Guam.

But the main business was, they decided, to be representing adult actresses. This was an industry, Ena learned, which generates twice as much money as

Coca-Cola, but which requires about a hundred thousand new girls every year, so there was always going to be work for an agent.

It has to be focused on America, though. In Britain they'll only pay a girl £200 a day. And the industry here isn't as clean; you can't be so sure that the other actors have been properly tested for STDs.

What the Los Angeles producers want is fresh-looking English girls for bit parts – to take part in sex scenes. Classic boy–girl stuff. They already have the big stars, but there's a need for new girls in the support roles.

There are always movies being made. If you go out there, work hard and shoot two movies a day you can work for two weeks and come home with $20,000 – minus 15 per cent for Ena's agency.

There were set-up costs. Ena and Mali were almost out of cash, worrying whether they were really doing the right thing, when the phone finally started ringing.

The first time they sent some girls to LA, Ena flew out there in advance to hook them up with the producers. Some of the girls never showed. They just took the free flight and then scarpered.

Luckily Ena and Mali had some other girls on their books and were able to send them out five days later so they didn't blow it completely. Now they make the girls buy their own tickets and refund them when they return.

When they received their first cheques from America it was – wow! Up until then this had just been a dream in Ena's head. Friends had worried that she was throwing her journalism degree down the pan. Now it was working out. It felt great.

But it's tough finding the women. In the early days they would approach them in the street. 'Sorry if you think we're being too up front, but have you ever thought of a career in the glamour industry?'

These days they just go out in the evenings with flyers: *'Become a porn star'*; *'Lapdance across the world'*.

Being a girl makes it easier to recruit other girls. It makes them feel safer. They know she's not some sleazy character on the pull.

Sometimes the boyfriends call up. 'My girl will do it, but only with me.'

Yeah, yeah.

But then you get the genuine ones. They phone up hesitantly, saying, 'I've had this leaflet lying around for a couple of weeks, and...'

Mali and Ena tell them to send photos. Then they interview them a couple of times. Ask them what they want to do. If they're up to it, they say, 'We're going to do a little showreel of you doing some solo action stuff on the bed.'

Then they tell them to visit an STD clinic and come back with the certificates to show that they're clean.

Talking frankly about sex becomes normal. It's an everyday task. Other people talk about their nine-to-fives. She has to talk about sex.

They've learned a few hard lessons. Some girls lose their nerve the day before they're supposed to fly. 'Oh... ah, my dad's very ill.'

It can be stressful, desperately trying to find the six girls a producer is asking for. She'll have sleepless nights as a deadline approaches. 'Oh no, what am I going to do?'

But Ena is remarkably determined. Mali has suggested a few other niches. They have some dominatrixes on their books now; your normal puppy training, corporal punishment, wax torture, nipple torture.

Mali and Ena – who're both half Filipina – also do what they advertise as 'a geisha limousine service' for stag and birthday parties. They pour drinks. Ena feeds the men grapes and dances around in high heels while Mali rubs the men's necks. It's not easy to dance in a cramped limo. It's given her strong thighs. She ends up doing a lot of writhing. For two hours they pamper the men while the limo drives around the city.

All in all the business is going well. For a start, she's already managed to pay off her £12,000 student loan for that journalism course.

15

Soon it will be the end of everything

TEN COMMANDMENTS yard signs. In Deuteronomy 6: 3–9, God promises to bless those who obey and display his commandments... 'that ye may increase mightily, and thou shalt write them upon the posts of thy house'. We make all types yard signs. T-shirts. Wholesale prices. Discount to conservative candidates. [illegible]. $2 wholesale

In Montgomery, Alabama, the state's Supreme Court Chief Justice is on trial. Again.

Eight years ago, Judge Roy Moore was just an obscure judge in a small Alabama county. He's a Vietnam vet who enjoyed woodworking as a hobby.

One day, using a hot soldering iron, he burned the Ten Commandments into a hinged wooden tablet and put it up in his courtroom in Etowah County, right behind his courtroom bench.

Moore starts court sessions with a prayer.

When in 1994 the American Civil Liberties Union objected, Moore claimed he was the victim of religious persecution. Conveniently he was at the time standing for election as a circuit judge.

The Christian citizens of Etowah County rallied behind him and obscure outsider Judge Moore was duly elected.

As the years roll on, Judge Moore's refusal to remove the Ten Commandments from his courthouse has developed into a mammoth, drawn-out legal battle.

So far the only winner appears to be Moore himself.

In 2000, proclaiming himself 'The Ten Commandments Judge', Roy Moore stood for the Republican candidacy in the election for Chief Justice of the Alabama Supreme Court. Moore's a robust right-wing Christian, a man who states publicly that homosexuality is 'an inherent evil'.

Vern Bearden was one of the many who helped Roy Moore with that campaign.

Vern's a jolly, quiet-spoken, well-educated 50-year-old civil servant with five children, who lives in the small Huntsville, Alabama, suburb of Owens Crossroads.

Vern makes yard signs – small plastic printed signs that you plant in your front lawn. He started in 1999, back when Alabama was voting on whether there should be a state lottery.

He's always been a conservative Christian. A Presbyterian and a dedicated member of the right-wing Christian Coalition, Vern objected to the lottery on biblical grounds. Not only does gambling exploit the poor but it inspires people to put their faith in luck rather than God.

The pro-lottery lobby had big money and was clearly ahead in the polls. But soon you could see Vern's 'No Lottery' yard signs all over. In October 1999, swayed by the religious right's grass-roots campaign, voters about-faced and rejected the lottery.

Now Vern looked around for something else to make yard signs about. That was when he hit on the Commandments. He thinks what Judge Roy Moore is doing is great.

For Vern, the Ten Commandmants are one of the most important scriptures in the Bible – if not the most important. He thinks they would have been very important to the Founding Fathers too. They came here to found a Christian nation. In law, that's what it should be.

If the ACLU were intent on removing the Commandments, they were morally wrong, he felt, and he would replace them.

In 2000, Vern put one of the first he made on his own lawn, facing on to the Old 431 Highway, where it sits to this day. He made five hundred altogether.

They sold out.

He made another thousand.

They went too.

When Judge Moore came to Owens Crossroads, Vern met him. They held a banquet for him. Vern's children played the music at the banquet. Vern says he's a quiet man, very soft spoken, but with strong feelings behind that quietness.

Vern made the yard signs for Moore's election at a special low price. He helped campaign too. Across the state Moore erected big billboards saying: 'Upholding the Moral Foundation of the Law' and 'Upholding the Ten Commandments'.

'I am a judge who did not bend the knee to the liberal ACLU,' said Roy Moore, 'and I have stood up for the people...'

On the day of the Republican primary to choose their candidate, Vern watched the results come through on TV. They were nervous. It was a gamble. The four other candidates were better funded. The leading candidate had raised $2 million.

A lot of people in the Christian community hadn't wanted Moore to run. If he lost, it would be a major blow to the conservative Christians; it would be devastating to the Ten Commandments movement.

But Moore won by a sizeable majority and went on

to beat the Democratic candidate. Vern isn't a party person, but when it was announced that Judge Moore had been elected, the Bearden household was jubilant. And relieved.

But Judge Roy Moore had another surprise up his sleeve. Six months after taking office, he secretly prepared a 2.5-ton granite monument inscribed with the Commandments and – in the dead of night – wheeled it into the Alabama court rotunda and left it there.

It sat there, squat and grey. The top is carved to look like an open Bible. Down the side, in black letters, are the words of the Commandments. A big *so there* to all the liberals.

Incensed, the ACLU and the Southern Poverty Law Center – a group more accustomed to prosecuting KKK members – have taken Moore to court again on behalf of non-Christians and other Americans who feel the legislature is being hijacked.

Somewhere in the house his youngest son is playing on the grand piano. His eldest child won first place in piano and violin competitions all over Alabama. Vern is proud that he is now Concert Master at Pensacola Christian College in Florida, where they teach that God created the world in six days, and that man chose sin, and that the return of Christ is imminent.

As the Roy Moore issue hots up all over America, Vern's less ostentatious Ten Commandments yard signs continue to sell. A woman in Norwalk, California, orders two hundred a month and passes them around her neighbourhood. A man in Wichita, Kansas, sells them at a booth at state fairs.

Every time the ACLU initiates another case against a town or state displaying the Ten Commandments – in Kentucky, Indiana or Florida – his sales soar. Churches in Jacksonville and Orlando have just ordered several hundred more.

Then there are the Ten Commandments bumper stickers. A local Christian gave him the money to print up forty thousand of them. He gave ten thousand to the Christian Coalition to distribute and they've sent them out to supporters. All over Alabama there are cars driving around with his stickers on their fenders.

The Ten Commandments Judge has become a national rallying cry for the conservative right. In years to come he will eventually be stripped of his post as the Supreme Court Judge of Alabama by a federal judicial ethics panel, but this will only increase the sense of outrage among his followers. On Christian talk shows, Judge Moore will fulminate loudly against the tyranny of liberalism. There is talk that some day Roy Moore may even make presidential candidate – a kind of Ralph Nader of the Christian right.

In the meantime, Vern is fulfilled by his work as a foot-soldier for Roy Moore's Ten Commandments movement. He is accomplishing something purposeful, and he's enjoying that. It gives his life meaning.

Soon he is going to reach twenty-five thousand. His mark-up is enough to pay for advertising, but that's about all. Recently the ACLU sued the small town of Franklington, Louisiana, for putting up a sign that read 'Jesus Is Lord over Franklington'.

Inspired, Vern has printed up his own 'Jesus Is Lord' yard signs. He's sending out the first of them this week.

Sometimes he wonders where he gets his combative side from. He thinks he's maybe a descendant of the Levites – the Jews Moses entrusted with the care and protection of the Tabernacle.

It's his ministry; making and selling these 18″ x 24″ pieces of plastic.

MY NAME is Michael Leon and I am seeking to communicate with individuals interested in the paranormal, especially UFOs and alien races. I would also like to communicate with others regarding the NWO

He lives alone on Long Island and works as an office clerk for a small company in Manhattan. In his spare time he goes for walks, or to the beach. He is a prolific reader.

He remembers reading Erich von Däniken's *Chariots of the Gods* – the best-seller that claimed that the ancient Earth had been visited by aliens – at the age of 11 or 12. He was always interested in UFOs but couldn't understand why the media didn't give them much attention.

He's 39 now, and in recent years he's come to understand why that is. He's slowly starting to learn the truth. There's been a lot of cover-up.

It's a conspiracy. They don't really want the truth to come out. Because it goes against their plan. Why things are the way things are. Why the money system is the way it is.

The world is going to be changing soon. There will be great physical changes – the likelihood is that there will be a pole shift. The people who are running the world are trying to put a global dictatorship in place by 2012 so that they can maintain control when it all happens.

This UFO/New World Order thing is really, really big.

He knows this from the books he's read. A few years ago he became interested in the works of Zecharia Sitchin – a ufologist who claims to be an expert in translating Sumerian texts. In books like *The 12th Planet* and *The Lost Book of Enki* he tells of a hidden planet, Nibiru, whose orbit takes it close to Earth every 3,600 years. Nibiru is peopled by a reptilian extra-terrestrial species, the Anunnaki, who helped create the human race. More than likely, Adam and Eve were creations of the Anunnaki.

Nibiru is coming around again soon.

Most people are unaware of this. But you know something? It's very, very exciting when you're finding out about it for the first time.

Last March, Michael went to a lecture in Boston given by David Icke. He always looks forward to Icke's visits to the USA. His books trace the reptilian blood lines of the ancient extra-terrestrial visitors. They interbred with humans and created descendants who became rulers and presidents through the ages. Icke shows how they're controlling our governments and our institutions. Even the Windsors have reptilian ancestry.

He's interested in what Icke has to say in his new book that's coming out soon: *Alice in Wonderland and the WTC Disaster.*

He was working in his office ten blocks away from the World Trade Center on September 11. When he was told to evacuate the building, it took him five hours to get home because none of the trains and buses was running. The attack surprised him, but when he did more research he started to understand the connections.

Right when George W. Bush became President, that told him the world was heading for something – if you know anything about the Bush family.

The Bush family, the Windsor family – they're all related. The Bush family even financed Hitler's rise to power in the 1930s, according to the books he's read. These people want the nations of the world to go to war – that way they'll increase their control.

Michael doesn't talk about all this with his family. They're not ready to understand it. They scoff at it.

Occasionally he meets someone at a UFO conference and they strike up a friendship. The other day he was on the subway when he spotted someone reading

David Icke's *Children of the Matrix* and he struck up a conversation.

But it's not easy to find people who share his views. He wouldn't talk to co-workers about it. He doesn't try to force it down people's throats.

Some people think he's weird. He gets a little excited when he does talk about it, but that's only because he's so passionate about it.

You know you keep hearing about missing children? What he's found out is that the CIA are playing a big part in that. The missing children have been scooped up. They're what you call mind-control slaves.

He says to people, 'I'm not making any of this up. I've done a lot of research and reading about this.'

Over the years he's built up a circle of four or five people with whom he corresponds. They share his frustration that most people aren't ready to hear about how we're moving inch by inch towards a global dictatorship. The people who are running the world are trying to get that in place before 2012.

He placed the advert to try to find new people to talk about all this with. Only one person has answered it so far. She's a lady who lives in Utah. Like Michael, she's a prolific reader. And she, too, believes in the New World Order conspiracy. But she doesn't take the UFO thing very seriously.

'Well,' she says, 'how do we know UFOs are real?'

She thinks they're a hoax, created by the government to mask what they're really doing.

He's called her a couple of times. She seems like a nice lady, but she is part of the Patriot movement. They think the conspiracy is part of a plan to destroy the white race. He doesn't see it that way.

'No,' Michael argues. 'It's a plan to *enslave* the human race.'

She thinks it's a national conspiracy, not a global one. Some people don't see the bigger picture.

He probably won't call her again.

YOU HAVE TRIED ALL ELSE, NOW TRY JESUS. HE IS ALIVE AND HEARS YOUR WORDS OF HELP. ALICE SPRINGS [illegible] SON POWER AND LIGHT

Jim was the sort of American who thought he was going to run the world. He'd graduated from engineering school, was doing a Masters in business and was planning to start law school after that.

Everything was going well. He was married. He had a beautiful young son. Yet the exhilaration of each new achievement never seemed to last. He felt unfulfilled; something was missing.

He drank. He slept around. One night twenty-one years ago he bought a bunch of drugs, went to a party and almost cheated on his wife again.

Instead he got in the car and drove home down the tree-lined road. It was raining heavily. On a dark road in Oregon he cried out to the Lord for a sign: 'If you reveal yourself to me,' he pleaded, 'if you show yourself, I will follow you.'

Nothing happened.

But when he woke up the next morning, somehow his whole life was different.

'I guess I didn't understand it at the time,' says Jim. 'But what it was was I was born again. The spirit of God came into my life.'

At 26 his ambition vanished. His whole attitude changed. Instead he listened to the Spirit.

Though his wife was born again too, the marriage didn't last. They split up.

The Spirit talks to him. He says it'll do that if you listen. You just start hearing the word and doing what He wants. Sometimes the Spirit tells him to move on. It can be pretty specific.

Ten years ago it told him to go to Australia. He moved to Perth and worked there for a few years. He's an engineer and can pick up work pretty much wherever he goes.

A little while ago he felt the Spirit was leading him to the most central place in Australia. It was important that he go to the very middle.

It wasn't as if he just jumped into his car and drove; he spent three months carefully planning the move to Alice Springs. He doesn't know the exact reason why he was called there. He says he'll know when it happens, whenever that may be.

Alice is a rough city. Raw. He has his own place up in what they call the Gap – a pass in the mountain range. Aborigines who aren't allowed to drink in the camps they live in come into town. They sit outside the store on the other side of the street, screaming and yelling.

It's desert. It's kind of beautiful in its own way. Some days he misses the rain and the green and the cold of Oregon. It hasn't rained here for eight months.

The drought is the worst in Australia's history. Jim takes note. All events these days seem to be 'the worst ever', 'the driest ever', 'the biggest ever'.

Soon it will be the end of everything. All the signs have been fulfilled.

The final one was Israel becoming a nation. The Bible says that will be the last generation before He returns.

From Alice Springs, Jim watches the craziness getting worse and worse – the World Trade Center and Iraq. The craziness is everywhere. Things are deteriorating rapidly.

He doesn't talk about this to the people he works with here. He's not a big talker. He has a fear of man in him. If he knows you're a born-again Christian, then it's simpler for him. But strangers aren't easy to talk to.

He likes Alice because it's small. You see the same people from day to day.

But he doesn't really have friends. He hangs out by himself most of the time, keeps himself to himself.

That's why he put the adverts in the local classified magazine. It's his way of telling people what he's found. Of spreading the ministry without having to talk to people.

The newspaper says he has to put a phone number in. They won't print it unless you do. But no one ever calls anyway.

16
The dressing-up box

• **DISNEY DRESSING UP**, genuine Disney shop dressing up clothes sadly outgrown, Alice in Wonderland, Jasmine 4–6yrs, Minnie Mouse, Cinderella, Snow White 6–8yrs, each £8 pam@ [illegible] / [illegible] 6–10pm eves and w/e

When Pam Scanlon was 8 her father bought her a wedding dress.

It was a Christmas present. There was a bridal-wear sale at the Army & Navy store in Liverpool, and they were selling the gowns for the knock-down price of fifteen shillings. A neighbour across the road said she wanted one for her daughter too, so Pam's dad called them up and asked, 'If I buy two can I have them for ten shillings each?'

They went the next day. Pam gazed at the fantastic dresses – about ten or twelve of them – hanging on a rail in the entrance to the shop.

Pam remembers, as she stood there with her father, all the sales ladies coming down the stairs, and out of the manageress's office. Word had spread; everyone wanted to take a peek at the man who wanted to buy two wedding dresses.

In the end, he managed to buy them both for a pound. The dress Pam chose was, she remembers, dreadfully fluffy and way too big for her – she must have trampled it to pieces, wearing it – but she loved it. The dress was kept in her dressing-up box, along with discarded ball gowns and other oddments.

It was natural that when she had children of her own, Pam would make a dressing-up box for them too.

Pam's favourite was the Alice in Wonderland they bought for their eldest girl, Hannah. There weren't Disney shops in Britain then. They bought it on a family holiday in Disney World. And when Hannah wanted a Minnie Mouse costume for Christmas, Pam sewed one, copying from a photo they'd taken on holiday.

Tim, their second child, had Robin Hood. Pam also made him a Superman outfit when he was 5 – and when he was about 7 she sewed chains and studs on to an old leather jacket so he could look like John Travolta. Pam would have stopped after two children, but her husband wanted more; they ended up with four girls and one boy.

Each had their favourite Disney costumes. One girl was Snow White, another was Jasmine, and so on. They kept the outfits in a big chest upstairs, and after school they'd disappear into their rooms, get dressed up and come down laughing.

But Hannah's in her last year at Newcastle University now, and the youngest girl is 9. In the run-up to Christmas, Pam decided it was time to clean out the box to make way for all the new clutter that would be arriving in a few weeks.

The dressing-up box is pretty much empty now. They've just kept the best stuff to sell. The 9-year-old wanted to hang on to the Disney clothes. But when she tried to squeeze into them she discovered that they didn't fit any more.

With the children growing up, Pam returned to work as a midwife.

She had to catch up with a Return to Practice course. It was nerve-racking. When she was younger it was just, 'Oh, yeah. I can do that.'

Now, with five children of her own, she understands what children mean to you. She thinks about how – if something went wrong – the parent would have to live with that for ever. She looks at the first-time mothers and thinks, They haven't got a clue what's coming to them... But then nobody has.

Most years they still fly back to Disney World for a

holiday with the younger ones. They've been there umpteen times. They tried going to Las Vegas, but missed Disney World too much. Pam still gets a buzz the first time they go through the gates and feel the Florida sun beating down on them.

She likes Space Mountain best. There, she says, she can be a big kid again.

• **ANN SUMMERS It's glitz. It's glamourous. It's 100% girlie, parties arranged, also jobs available now. Call**

She's doing one next Saturday in Cardiff. Joanne says it's a lot of fun. People are up for a laugh. They wouldn't be having an Ann Summers party unless they were, would they?

She does between one and five a week. OK, sometimes you get a tough crowd. Last week she was in a room full of women, all sitting there with their arms crossed; she was thinking, I don't believe this is happening to me.

It only takes a couple of drinks, though, and people open up. That and the party games. Joanne usually plays Pass the Vibrator, where you have to slip it down your clothes and then pass it to the next person. Then there's the Blowjob Game, where you inflate a condom sitting on a foot pump, bouncing up and down. If she hasn't broken the ice by the Blowjob Game, then nothing will do it.

After the games, she goes through the catalogue. She usually does well on the play outfits too, like the nurse's outfit ('make his temperature soar') at £29.99

or 'The Wench' at £31.99. And there's 'The Kizzy's at £12.99. They've got peep-hole bras and crotchless knickers and so on.

And there are the sex toys. They're much easier to sell now than when she started. Often as not the girls have already used them.

'I got one,' someone will say.

'Really? Well, I'm getting one too, then.'

Half the job has already been done by the TV. Since the Rampant Rabbit – £26.99, 'ensures maximum clitoral stimulation' – was on *Sex and the City* she's sold hundreds of them. And the Pulsatron (£35.99) sells well, 'cause it's got the bits to go on the men too. So you can use it together. That was on *Sex Tips for Girls.*

At a good party she'll sell around £300 worth; the company says organizers make an average of around £45 a party. Joanne has most of the items in the catalogue hanging in her own closet. She discovered early on she didn't sell so much unless she had the stuff herself. Her boyfriend seems happy. There's a lot of stuff she has he likes.

Sometimes things can get a bit wild, especially when they're drunk. She was throwing a party in a pub in Newport for about thirty girls and this girl playing the Blowjob Game was laughing so much she peed herself and then told everyone. Not that she needed to.

You could see she had.

MURDER MYSTERIES
Tel:
Fax:

Even today, with a bit of hair dye, Sean passes for the Handsome Hero.

Today, at the Charnwood Hotel, Sheffield, he is playing the Inspector.

He has been doing murder mysteries for ten years.

As an actor his break never quite came. Being an amorous young lad, he had married young. It's not easy supporting five kids through pier shows and musicals. He's driven taxis, forklifts, even a Mother's Pride delivery van. But when he's not performing he feels inadequate.

Once he really thought he'd made it when Ken Loach cast him in his TV movie about privatised railway workers, *The Navigators*. The producer said, 'Don't worry, Sean. A lot will be happening when this is finished.'

But it didn't.

He was up for a Pot Noodles advert the other day, but he didn't get it.

Instead he's made a business producing his own nostalgic musical stage shows, with names like *Stage Door Memories*, or *The Blitz*.

Then he heard a hotel manager he knew complaining he was being charged £1,000 for a murder mystery evening.

'My God. I could do that for half.'

'You're on,' said the manager.

He's been doing it for ten years, now. Sean hires local celebrities, musicians and actors to fill the parts. It irks him that one of his former actors has gone off on his own to set up his own murder mysteries company in competition. It's not the loss of talent he regrets – 'He was about as scary as a blancmange' – it's the betrayal. 'It's stabbing me in the back,' says Sean.

His speciality is the musical murder mystery. It goes like this. Entertainers from a nearby holiday camp have pulled off an audacious robbery, agreeing to meet up at a local hotel to split the loot, only to find that their room is pre-booked by dinner guests.

The Inspector, who he plays himself, is on hand to solve the crime.

The trick is to make it fun, but also believable.

Tonight it has been perhaps a little too believable. Halfway through dinner, the Victim stood, clutched his throat and staggered out of the room. His car was deliberately parked outside the dining-room window.

The actor tottered towards it, managed to get the door open, but then slumped, dead, over the steering wheel, car horn blaring.

Unfortunately unsuspecting onlookers from across the road had witnessed this too. They hurried to assist what they assumed was a dying man.

But now it's the end of the evening and the audience are asking questions before they attempt to finger the Murderer.

There is always one person who tries to be clever. Tonight it's a woman. 'Excuse me,' she interrupts. 'How come I've just seen the dead man drinking in the bar next door?'

'Madam,' says Sean, haughtily, 'I was asked to play Long John Silver in *Treasure Island*, but I didn't have to have my effin' leg off.'

There is laughter.

Applause.

There is no feeling like it.

Wanted new members, for our friendly re-enactment group of the Wild West, if interested please phone Duncan or June on [illegible] evenings after 6pm

'Right,' somebody will decide. 'We'll do a bank raid today.'

And so that's what they do. The Texas Rangers A Division of Hemel Hempstead. Or they'll do a jail break, shooting off their Colt .45s at each other.

They've been doing it long enough to know who're the bad guys and who the goodies. Duncan's been a Texas Ranger for fifteen years. Before that he was one of the Watford Outlaws.

It started when he and his brother saw a small Wild West group performing on the Isle of Wight.

That, thought Duncan, is something that I want to get into. Right there and then he bought himself a double-rig gunbelt with Mexican toolwork.

But he didn't take it any farther until one night he and his brother were at a pub disco when the Watford Outlaws came in on a pub raid, all dressed in the gear, rattling charity pots for some good cause.

Duncan and his brother joined up. That's how Duncan met June. She was a Watford Outlaw too. Her dad was one of the men who'd set up the Outlaws. He's been doing this for getting on for thirty years, originally as one of a group called the Chiltern Cowboys.

But the Outlaws were a small group who did only a few shows every summer. The Texas Rangers had been going a couple of years when they invited the Outlaws to join up with them. Duncan hasn't looked back.

There's around twenty of them. Most are lorry drivers, like Duncan. June works at the checkout at Tesco's. There's a glazier and a couple of cleaners. Even a solicitor.

When Duncan and June married ten years ago they had a full Southern-style ceremony. Duncan dressed up in Confederate uniform. (There's a shop called the Sutlers Store in Bournemouth which specializes in selling anything you'd ever want for a Civil War re-enactment.) He rode to church on horseback. June arrived in a carriage wearing a white ball gown.

They've two kids now, girls, 8 and 10, who love to do the shows too. Every group has its own style. There's a place called Laredo in Kent – a static site where they've built a small town of storefronts – and they've chosen a year in the 1860s as their theme. Some groups go for all the fancy line-dancing gear. Duncan's not into that.

'Only dancin' I like is at the end of a rope,' he says.

The Rangers like to keep it basic. Duncan wears a duster coat, like the one Clint Eastwood wears, and under that, granddad shirts. He has a genuine Model 94 Winchester – made in 1894 – which he picked up for £150 a few years back.

There are groups all over the country. The Lawmen of Bristol. The Arizona Rangers of Bradford. The Whisky Creek Club of Pulborough. The Missouri Rangers of Lincolnshire. Duncan's favourite is the Spirit of the West – they operate in a fixed Western town near Newquay run by a guy called JB who looks a bit like Lee Van Cleef with long hair. Duncan used to go down there to help him out with the gunfights.

It's the storefronts which the Rangers specialize in. Duncan and his brother have built a whole mobile set which includes one 24-foot two-storey building. They'll turn up at a showground on a Friday night and camp out cowboy-style with the whole family. It'll take them six or seven hours to set the storefronts up.

July is pretty busy. This weekend the Rangers are doing a small show at London Colney. They charge £250, which covers their costs and leaves £50 over to give to the disabled charity they support. Spending the weekend under canvas, getting dirty and smelly, really helps Duncan get into the part – especially if he's playing a baddie.

He never gets tired of it. The moment he puts the clothes on he can forget all the hassle of the week, driving his lorry.

He steps out into the arena with his guns, his hat and his coat, and it all disappears.

Felice Kaplan – a 44-year-old West Hollywood divorcee – keeps promising her son Brandon she'll get a job. He's 14.

Felice has just never been the sort of girl who can wear pantyhose and dresses and go to the office every day. She always winds up telling the boss to go fuck himself.

Three weeks ago she was dressing up as a hot dog, waving to cars to attract custom to a food stand, and shouting, 'I'll relish this moment for ever.' Or, 'Don't touch my buns.'

She likes the attention.

The week after that she answered an ad in the *LA Weekly* that turned out to be for a job calling up auto tool shops to sell the mechanics porno movies. 'We have anal and three-way penetration. Which one would you like to purchase today?'

Halfway through the interview she thought, This is so disgusting!, and asked them to excuse her, saying she had to go and put some more money in the meter.

She never went back.

This week she's answered this advertisement looking for female streetfighters. It turns out the company is making a DVD called called *Extreme Chickfights*. It's unlicensed fighting – 'no holds barred', boasts the organizer – usually filmed in someone's back yard. You get $50 if you fight and $150 if you win, they tell her. Felice is looking for quick cash.

This could be a fun thing, she tells herself.

This Saturday's fight is in a club on Melrose and Curzon, just four and a half blocks from where Felice lives. They've set up a ring there.

They want the girls to dress up for the fights. They want them to look sexy. One girl's turned up wearing a glittery outfit; another is wearing cute little doily panties.

Felice arrives dressed as a banana. It's a costume she wore so as to stand out when she went for the NBC game show *Let's Make a Deal*. She didn't get it. She did once win big on *The Price Is Right*, though.

She starts getting butterflies when she sees some of the other fighters. They look so dykey and strong. She is going to die. But here she is, joking to the people with video cameras interviewing each contestant, 'This banana isn't going to split...'

Thankfully Felice is paired up with a sweet-looking 21-year-old called Deena from Ventura. A nice little city. I could be her mother, thinks Felice.

She watches the other fights.

They scare her. These people are really hitting each other. Now she thinks she's going to die. She doesn't say that to Brandon, though, who's come with her to watch.

The Moroccan Princess is preparing to go up against the Sugar Princess from Detroit.

'I fight guys,' boasts the Sugar Princess.

'What?' taunts the olive-skinned girl with hair in corn braids under her boxing helmet. 'Do guys go easy on you?'

Elle Nucci is the sort of girl schoolfriends would call up when they wanted to scare people. She's actually part Italian, part Moroccan. You could mistake her for a Latina. Even in elementary school she enjoyed fighting. From the sixth grade she'd draw crowds after school at Kittridge Elementary, in the San Fernando Valley; forty people or more watching her get into it. She can still do it.

There's a click in her head and she just starts punching. Especially when there's some girl talking a lot of shit. Like a couple of years ago, when this girl in Vegas cussed her out. She'd been put up to it by Elle's ex-boyfriend. She didn't have a clue what hit her.

She enjoys fighting, but until recently she'd never trained. Four years ago she started training with a local gym. Her trouble is that despite all the boxing training the click in her head happens and she just starts throwing punches wildly, like she did at school.

She trains in the day; by night she works as a cashier at a local strip club.

The Sugar Princess is saying, loud enough for her to hear, 'I'm gonna kick her ass.'

Elle is quiet before a fight. She just says, 'Talk is cheap.'

Next thing they're in the ring. Elle waits to see what she's got. The Sugar Princess is fast, but her punch is weak. 'Is that all she's got?'

Elle is in charge from the start. In the first two rounds her opponent only manages to hit her maybe four times, while all the time Elle is pummelling her. In the third round, after three minutes and forty-six seconds, the Sugar Princess stops the fight.

It's an amazing feeling, being up there with the small crowd screaming. And winning. That's the best.

She's won the money too. She's going to use it to buy herself a new comforter set – a set of bedclothes.

Then there's Torley Allison.

Torley has fought a few bouts now. She's never lost yet. People recognize her when she arrives at the club. Torley doesn't like the attention.

She hates the fighting but needs the money. She's a jobless African-American, a single parent who's hoping that this fight club will take off so she doesn't have to look for a nine-to-five. That way she can spend more time with her 1-year-old boy.

She's a formidable fighter. Last time she took on two girls at once in a back-yard brawl for *Extreme Chickfights* and still won. It felt kind of weird, fighting in someone's back yard.

She's trained in tae kwan do. She never hit anyone in the face in her life before *Extreme Chickfights*. She's not used to it. She doesn't like to go for the faces. She doesn't like it, either, when she sees what happens when a punch connects with a face.

She wins again tonight and gets the money, but she never walks away from these events feeling good.

Now it's Felice's turn to step into the ring with Deena.

'I won't hurt you,' promises Deena, cutely.

Her opponent weighs in at only 145 pounds. Right now, Felice feels pretty cocky about the $150 prize. Maybe she can win after all.

But then the bell goes and suddenly Deena is beating the shit out of Felice, hitting her head again and again.

It's like those Gene Kelly movies, thinks Felice. Mm, you say, that dancing looks easy – until you do it yourself and fall on your face.

She just keeps hitting her.

Even wearing boxing headgear, each time Deena pounds her head she's seeing lights and stars, as if she's in a Warner Brothers cartoon. Bright lights. Swear to God. It's weird.

Stop it, I'm scared now!

Felice just can't get the hang of it. She tries to return the hits, but every time she pulls her fist back to swing it, Deena sees that she's wide open and punches her right in the face. Pow-pow-pow.

She's the daughter of a Jewish woman who escaped Hitler on the *Kinder* transport, who went on to join the British army. One of her brothers is a doctor. The other lives a good life in Israel. Everyone in her family has done well apart from her. 'Me?' says Felice. 'I'm just a fuck-up.'

The next day her shoulder hurts like hell. She's surprised to discover that she has no real bruises, though.

But then on Wednesday, her shoulder still hurting, the woman who runs *Extreme Chickfights* calls her up. 'Do you want to do it again?'

Felice thinks for a while. She says, 'You know? I think I might.'

He is Britain's fourth-most eccentric man.

According to the award he once won, that is.

He's still got the award; it's quite an accolade. It was presented by Sir Norman Wisdom.

You can see the cuttings about it with all the others, on the walls of Bean Central.

That's what he calls his flat on the Sandfields estate in Port Talbot. He has painted the walls baked-bean orange, and there he displays his collection of baked-bean rarities, including a massive HP baked beans shop display which you can look at while sitting in his inflatable orange chairs.

His girlfriend of almost thirteen years, Cheryl, isn't planning on moving in. She has her own place.

Barry Kirk always believed he'd been put on this planet for a reason. He was, he says, a bit of an individual – even at school. An oddball who enjoyed attention; who wanted people to know who he was. And never to forget it.

But when he left school he just did what every male used to do in those days. Chased the women and got drunk, basically. And got a job. He was a BP computer operator for thirteen years, all the time thinking, There's got to be something better than this.

Then he discovered charity fund-raising – the world of what he calls 'zany stunts'. Like dressing up as an angel and pushing a shopping trolley from Cardiff to Port Talbot, which he did once. He used to dress up as Eddie the Eagle and call himself Barry the Budgie. Plus he once got into the papers dressed up as a character he called Sir Knickerless Knight and sold knickers outside Tom Jones concerts: 'Why take yours off when you can buy them off me?' he shouted at the fans.

The baked-bean thing started in 1986 as an attempt to get into *The Guinness Book of Records*. One guy had lain in custard; another in spaghetti. Inspired by a photo of Roger Daltrey lying in beans on the cover of *Who Sell Out*, Barry declared he would lie naked (save for a pair of Speedos), his head shaved, in a bath of baked beans for a hundred hours.

Immersed in Happy Shopper baked beans, Barry raised £2,000 for the mentally handicapped. Afterwards he wasn't able to so much as smell a baked bean for four years. It put him right off – though he's back to eating them now.

After the baked-bean bath, people in Port Talbot started calling him 'the bean man'. That's when Captain Beany – the superhero from the planet Beanus – came into being.

He quit work in 1991 and stood as Captain Beany in the Neath by-election, sharing the platform with Lord Sutch of the Monster Raving Loony Party.

'The great man himself,' says Beany, reverentially. 'He was such a character, Lord bless him.'

Now, just as he had the fund-raising bug, he's caught the political bug too. Since then he's stood in local elections, borough elections, nationally and for the Welsh Assembly, and even in Euro elections, 'as a Eurobean candidate, ha ha ha'.

He has his own political party, the New Millennium Bean Party. His manifesto is that the government should give more money to charity. He's the treasurer; he's got a colleague who acts as his nominating officer; Cheryl acts as the secretary; a friend who does his PR also acts as his political agent, and the friend's wife sews his costumes.

Apart from marking his entry into politics, 1991 was

also the year his life as mere Barry Kirk ended. He went to a solicitor and said: 'Right. From now on I want to relinquish my name.'

He announced: 'I'm changing my name by deed poll – or bean pole, ha ha ha.'

Since then he's been Captain Beany. He says he can't even remember who Barry Kirk was. Barry Kirk worked with computers; that's not very exciting.

Everything is now under Captain Beany. You can find him in the phone book under Captain Beany. The same goes for his bank account, his credit cards, even his passport – 'Surname: Beany, Given name: Captain' – with the photograph of him dressed in his Captain Beany sunglasses and his face and shaven head covered in the orange body paint. (He buys the orange paint in bulk from theatrical suppliers Charles Fox in London.)

With that passport he's travelled the world, making Jimmy Savile-style appearences at marathons in New York, Los Angeles, Boston, Dublin and Paris. 'I run like the wind,' he declares. 'Baked beans are my sauce of power, ha ha ha.'

He could tell you hilarious stories about going through immigration with his Beany passport and his Beany outfit on – or so he claims.

Occasionally he's invited to attend functions. He was booked on the Eurostar for its first train out of

Waterloo. An inaugural cermony kind of thing. Wandering down the train, he spotted Jeffrey Archer standing there with his son. Archer signed his Captain Beany comic colouring-in book for him.

'Hey,' said Captain Beany, 'do you mind if I have my photograph taken with you?'

That was great. Two political has-beans, standing together.

He's always doing stuff for charity. By raising money marathon running he sent a young sick girl to Disneyland. Stuff like that. He was a big admirer of Lady Diana. He feels he has something in common with her – the way she worked for charity. After she died he had her image tattooed on his right arm.

But his constant round of charity work wears him down sometimes. He'd love the resources to do more, but he can't. Sometimes it hits him hard. 'Not to put too fine a point on it,' he says, 'it has made me depressed. I'll be totally honest with you, I have been to see my local psychiatrist, ha ha ha ha, just to cheer me up, you know?'

And apart from a small appearance in an upcoming episode of *The Basil Brush Show* as Captain Farto, he's currently not working.

It's embarrassing, Captain Beany going to a job centre.

'Not much call for superheroes,' he explains, 'ha ha ha.'

He wants more. He's spent twenty-one years making money for others. He thinks that there should be a job for Captain Beany now. He wants to pursue his bean dream.

He imagines a line of Beany products. He thinks there's potential. Why, he ponders, haven't HP and Heinz called him up to help publicize their products?

'It's a wonder that they haven't,' he says.

Best of all, someone could start making Captain Beany baked beans. 'I would love that,' he says. 'That would be brilliant. Beantastic, as they say.'

17
Christmas

Both teachers, Darryl and his wife live in the residential suburb of Mondeor, Johannesburg. On their salaries, with a 4-year-old child, it's hard. Teachers don't earn a lot.

The money's usually gone by the end of the month. And there's Christmas coming and their son's birthday is in January.

That's why Darryl put the advert in. He has some of the natural attributes.

'I'm overweight,' he says, and laughs a big booming laugh that could also prove useful. Maybe he can earn some money and sweat away a couple of kilos wearing a cheap eighty-buck Santa suit in the South African midsummer.

It's not the first time he's been Santa. He used to play the part ten years ago. Back then Darryl lived in the township of Ennerdale, south of Johannesburg. According to National Party classifications he was coloured – of mixed African and European origins. Cape coloured – that's what they used to call them.

He left school in 1984 when there were no jobs, so he trained as a teacher. He's never regretted that decision, though he started teaching in 1988, at the time when violence in the townships was reaching a peak, a time when teachers were striking about conditions and the townships were riven by social unrest.

Darryl wasn't involved politically; he's not that sort of person. Instead he used to try to teach the kids cricket to give them self-esteem. The slogan ran, 'A child in sport is a child out of court'.

Darryl thinks that it may have been something to do with not having a father himself which made him want to start visiting orphanages and children's homes in his township back in 1991. His own father died of a burst appendix in 1968 when Darryl was two years old.

He was teaching primary: it was mainly the older schoolchildren who were getting directly caught up in

Helen prepares to leave. She's an instrumentation designer for a consultant engineering company. For a single South African woman she's very well paid, but she's prepared to give all that up and start from nothing again. She sells her house, boxes up her belongings and ships them to the UK. They can't find homes for their Great Dane or boxer so they have to have them put down. That was the most devastating part of all.

But then she applies for travel documents for herself and Dean, to allow him to enter Britain. They're told they need a document from Dean's father, giving Helen the authority to take his son to the UK.

Pál and Helen divorced seven months before Dean was born. He was a Hungarian refugee. It must be five years since she's heard from him.

In the beginning, Pál had always been good about birthday cards and phone calls; he'd always made out that he was crazy about his son. But then all communication had just stopped.

At the time, Dean had been upset; for a while his behaviour worsened. But in time he got over it.

With no idea how to get in touch with Dean's father Pál to ask his permission, Helen tries the Hungarian Social Club in Johnannesburg. 'Oh,' someone there says, 'he died. About three years ago.' Pál had gone back to Hungary for his father's funeral and died of a heart attack there.

Helen's first reaction is disbelief. She is numb for a week. Maybe they are playing a prank on her, because Pál doesn't want to be found. But as she returns to the club to quiz complete strangers she realizes the story is true.

OK, say the British embassy. We'll need a copy of his death certificate, then – or a South African court ruling saying she has total custody. But months pass and nothing happens. Her attorney is costing her an arm and a leg, and she's no farther along, because the courts want the death certificate too before they can move. The Hungarian embassy isn't helpful. Where was he born? they ask. They need a birthplace in order to retrieve a death certificate, they say. Helen doesn't know. She could have asked Pál's 96-year-old mother but the person she has been speaking to at the Hungarian Social Club says she died a few months after Pál.

She makes hundreds of phone calls – to agencies here and in Hungary. She contacts her MP, but she has to tread carefully asking for government help. She fears being seen as yet another white person on the so-called 'chicken run'.

She's given up hope she'll ever find the document that will let her leave with her son. She doesn't know what to do any more. It's not as if she can unpack and start over. Her furniture is in Wales, waiting. She phones her parents there every week.

They've got a bedroom ready for her. Christmas is approaching. The entire family in Wales has already bought them presents.

Now she shares a small room in her brother's house in Kempton Park with her son. Dean is still traumatized.

The South African papers are full of news of the latest hijacking. A grandmother, a mother and her baby, held up, the mother raped and then all three shot execution-style. Just for the hell of it.

Dean sleepwalks almost every night.

LOOKALIKES AGENCY
Fake Faces Lookalikes – Come and join today FREEPHONE
bookings@
The Granary Office,
Owston Ferry,

Nerys was working in the accounts department of a printing company in Preston when she decided to change her hair. It was down to her waist, and quite dark, but she said to the people at Toni & Guy, 'Do what you want with it.'

'Wow,' she said afterwards. 'Really nice.'

They'd put highlights in it and cut it into a kind of bob.

In the office they said, 'God. You remind me of Victoria Beckham.'

She wasn't that interested in Posh Spice and she doesn't know anything about football, so she didn't really know what she looked like. But when her colleagues showed her pictures in magazines she thought, Yeah. I do a bit.

Her best friend Julie said, 'Why don't I bring a camera into work tomorrow and we'll email a few pics off to the agencies and see what happens?'

So they did. And when she came back from a holiday with her mum in Las Vegas, there was a letter. 'We've taken you on to our books...'

'Oh my God!'

Her first job was a 40th birthday party at a community centre. All she had to do for her £50 was carry the cake in and say, 'Happy birthday.'

She was terrified. If you're Joanna Lumley or Del Boy it's easy, but if you're Victoria what do you do? Stand there, pout a bit and look a bit posh?

Her first big job was five whole days in Manchester. They had hired a David Beckham, a Liam Gallagher, a Curly Watts, a Ruud van Nistelrooy and Nerys to walk round the city for a week holding copies of the *News of the World*.

Oh my God, thought Nerys. I'm petrified. I can't go up to Manchester on my own. I'll be the only girl.

She went along and she loved it. It was brill. Just walking around holding a newspaper and getting paid for it.

When Nerys first saw the David Beckham she thought someone as good looking as that must be conceited.

He's going to be a right so-and-so, she told herself. She's a personality kind of girl. If somebody can't make her laugh then they've got no chance.

His name was Mathew. On the Thursday, Nerys and Mathew were told to hang out in Marks & Spencer – where Beckham had recently endorsed his own line of clothing. It was the first time they were alone together. At lunch, Mathew said, 'Do you want to go for a coffee before we venture back?'

'Yeah, OK.'

Oh my God, she thought. What are we going to talk about?

That was when Nerys first realized she quite liked him, because he was much more down to earth than she'd expected. Quite fancied him, really.

Later that day they all went to the big nightclub Tiger Tiger. They let them into the VIP area there just as if they were celebrities themselves. After a bit Mathew reached out and took Nerys's hand.

Later they were kissing.

There was a lot of alcohol.

After that they started working together as Posh and Becks. Mathew says it wouldn't feel right working with another Posh. With Nerys he can hold hands and kiss and it feels natural.

They've moved in together in Chester, where Nerys's mum and dad live. That meant moving away from Preston – so she had to give up her job in the printing company.

Oh my God, she thought. What if we don't get enough work? What if we don't get any?

She looks at other Posh lookalikes' websites and there are some really bad ones out there. 'How bad is she?'

But then maybe people look at her photo and think the same? Oh, she's crap.

It was slow at first, but it's built up. Now they don't have to worry about the phone ringing, because they know it will.

What they love is that they meet different people each week. From the contract it might look like a boring party meet-and-greet, but by the end they usually end up on the dance floor with the rest of them, drinking White Russians.

During the England vs Turkey game at the Stadium of Light in Sunderland they were employed to hang out in the directors' box. It was quite spectacular, them having the best seats and looking down at the real David Beckham on the pitch below them. Some of the fans noticed Nerys there too, dressed in her Posh-style baseball cap and denim jacket, and started pointing. This is what it must feel like for Victoria.

Like the time when some Japanese tourists started banging on the windows of the London restaurant they were working in so she'd turn for their photographs.

Sometimes Nerys feels she gets a glimpse of what it's like to be famous. She'd love the free Dolce & Gabbanas, but she's not sure she'd like the rest of it.

She watched that documentary recently about Posh and Becks. He'd been playing for Real Madrid and they were trying to drive away in their jeep, with all these people hammering on the windows.

Brooklyn was on the back seat. The poor kid was really screaming at the noise, and all the people crowded around, throwing drinks at the car and stuff.

And they were turning round trying to comfort him. 'It's OK, Brooklyn. They're just people.'

On Christmas Day Mathew handed her a wrapped box that was too flat to be the Burberry watch she had asked for.

She opened it. Inside was this big card. *Christmas wishes to my fiancée.* Hang on a minute.

There was a ring inside and he'd written, 'Will you marry me?'

She burst out crying.

'Well,' he said eventually. 'What's the answer?'

• **Christmas tree**, 15ft, magnificent artificial tree, suit home, school or business, cost £500 new, good condition, easy storage, accept £90.00 or very near offer.
4pm–10pm weekends

It was a new house, but built to look like an old barn conversion.

The developers called it French Farmhouse Style. At the front of the house was an open dining room, built as a conservatory with glass that went right up to the roof line.

Chrissie and her husband lived there for fifteen years. They never had children, which Chrissie reckons makes it all the more amazing she's so into Christmas decorations. Maybe it's because she's a big kid at heart. She used to treat herself to all the things she would have liked to have had as a child. Like an enormous rocking horse. And her Christmas tree.

The first year they moved into the big five-bedroomed house, she bought a real tree, just like she used to have when she was a child; except that this one was 16 feet tall. She likes Christmas decorations on a grand scale.

The tree was so big that dragging it in made a real mess of the place. She had to wipe mud off the walls, and afterwards there were all the needles to collect.

The next year she saw a 15-foot artificial tree in a garden centre. It was going cheap because it had already been on display in the cafeteria there. She had to buy it. It was a third off.

For fifteen years, that was her Christmas tree. It used to take about two days to assemble and dress, climbing up it with a stepladder or hanging from the galleried landing upstairs.

The decorations were different each year. Nice and tasteful. Not tacky. It wasn't that she spent a lot of money on them. She used to make fabric bows and buy stuff in the January sales. The decorations were usually going cheap because no one wanted the really gigantic ones that suited her tree. On holiday she'd find things from all over the world to go on it – not necessarily Christmas things.

People started coming round just to see what Chrissie's tree was like that year. There were complaints if it didn't go up on 1 December. It got to the point where she would pull the curtains to on 28 November so she had a couple of days to get it ready for the grand switch-on.

It's probably the last Christmas her mum spent with them before she died that Chrissie remembers best.

That year they had Christmas early, on the 10th, because her sister was going to be abroad on Christmas Day. And it snowed.

'Christmas is never the same when you've lost someone close, is it?'

And afterwards, in January, she'd have to dismantle it, which was quite a joke. She used to stow it in the loft, in about seven bin liners, all labelled to save it being too much of a fight to put it up again the next year.

When it came to helping, her husband wasn't much use. None whatsoever. That was the trouble with their marriage. It was always Chrissie who laid the patios, washed the cars and painted the outside of the house. He never did anything.

Towards the end she started suffering from ME. She believes it was stress related. Partly it was her job as a primary school teacher. But she thinks it didn't help that he never used to do anything around the house. With her ill, his laziness took its toll on the fabric of the house. It stopped looking nice.

They would have been married twenty-five years this August. She can't quite believe it herself. She should have done it about fifteen years ago now. It was his total lack of enthusiasm for anything which ended it.

When she was citing 'unreasonable behaviour' as the cause, one of the guys down the road said, 'Put down that time I came round and you were wheeling in four tons of aggregate and there he was, sitting on his bum in the garden.'

The divorce has just come through. They've sold the house. It had too many memories for her to want to stay on there. She bought a terraced house instead. She had to sell a lot of stuff because the place was so much smaller – such as her rocking horse.

But she never moved into it. Because she met Gary and moved into his semi instead.

Life is simple here. People have no pretensions. She's so happy; it's like going back to her roots.

Gary's the total opposite of her ex. He's the sort of man who – if she's not home quick enough – will have the tea on the table all ready for her when she arrives. After the previous twenty-five years, that's amazing.

She's already put the decorations up in his modest semi. 'Slow down!' he tells her.

This Christmas they're using the tree he's always had. It's more modest. She kept some of her favourite baubles for Gary's tree – the maroon ones. She's bought a new fairy for the top, because the one she had from the old tree is far too big. It's a fibre-optic one.

'I've never had one of those before,' she says. 'I'm learning to live with it.'

Acknowledgements

Thanks to all at the *Observer* who have helped, especially to Louise France for enthusing, Ian Tucker for remaining calm, and Allan Jenkins for saying yes. Thanks, too, to Penny Gardiner and Toby Mundy at Atlantic for seeing the point.